Famous
Woodstock Cooks
AND THEIR FAVORITE RECIPES

Joanne Michaels
Mary Barile

Dedication

For Nancy Michaels
      Ralph Barile &
         Cornelius Van Der Cort

Library of Congress Number 87-083370
ISBN 0-9619429-0-8

Acknowledgments

We are grateful to everyone in Woodstock who gave generously of their time to talk with us. Each person shared a unique story, which let us piece together this slice of the town's culinary history. A special thanks to Barry Samuels of The Golden Notebook, Joan Munkacsi and the Woodstock Library. Without everyone's enthusiasm, patience and personal involvement in this project, **Famous Woodstock Cooks** would have never been published.

Thanks . . . .

Contents

Introduction

To some, the name "Woodstock" still conjures up visions of the Sixties: flower children, long hair, tattered jeans, head shops, and a credo in which money was often in short supply but where there was plenty of peace and free love to go around. Ironically, Woodstock is now one of the most prosperous towns in the Hudson Valley, and its tradition of attracting creative people from all the arts continues. From the utopian arts colony that was founded in 1902 to the colorful community of rock musicians that emerged 60 years later, Woodstock has been home to such artists and entertainers as Yasuo Kuniyoshi, Doris Lee, Milton Avery, George Bellows, Joan Baez, Bob Dylan, Paul Butterfield and Todd Rundgren. And that doesn't even begin to cover the dancers, writers, actors and composers who enjoyed the town's tolerance and inspiration.

This tradition of tolerance dates back to 1787, when Woodstock was incorporated and settled by largely English, Dutch and German settlers. It became a lumber town, a glass factory center and a source of bluestone. In the 1870s, Woodstock was home to circus performers and actors, but it was in 1902 that a wealthy Englishman, Ralph Radcliffe Whitehead (a student of John Ruskin), his wife, Jane Byrd McCall, writer Hervey White and artist Bolton Brown founded the artists' colony of Byrdcliffe, which flourished until the early 1930s. Two years later, Hervey White added a nearby colony for writers and musicians and named it The Maverick to emphasize its free spirit. White had a theater built for summer chamber music concerts and visitors can still enjoy classical music there on Sunday afternoons in July and August. In 1915, White inaugurated the Maverick Festival, an event held each year on the night of the August full moon. There was music, dancing and staged performances by resident artists, who attracted audiences of several thousand costumed spectators. (Unfortunately, although costumed spectators are still found around Woodstock, the festival is not.)

But what about the world-renowned festival, the 1969 celebration of love in the Aquarian Age? The festival that made Woodstock a household name once again in this century? It didn't take place here. The town board voted against having so many people invade a village that had inadequate resources for handling large crowds. And so the festival was moved 50 miles southwest of the village green, to a dairy farm in Bethel, New York, where the name of Woodstock still clung to the posters and publicity material and the seeds of a legend were planted in mud.

A discussion of Woodstock shouldn't omit the fact that people have been drawn to the town over the years because of its extraordinary beauty. Surrounded by mountains, including imposing Overlook, Woodstock consists of 70 square miles and five hamlets in addition to the village itself: Bearsville, Shady, Lake Hill, Willow and Zena. We wanted to write a book about Woodstock that took readers behind the village green, down the back roads, up the hollows and into the hamlets to show that there is far more to the town and its people than what can be seen on Tinker Street during a Saturday afternoon. We wandered these areas in an attempt to uncover food traditions and it seemed to us that the best way to convey the "flavor" of the town and the diversity of its 7,000 people was through their food. What we discovered was an eclectic blend of farm cooking, Continental cuisine, low budget meals for "starving" artists, gourmet health food and exotic dishes from around the globe. Although we have included people we call "famous" Woodstock cooks (many are well known outside the community), many are "ordinary" citizens who are just as vital to the area's spirit.

It was easy to pinpoint the stars and town personalities while organizing this book, and many times one Woodstock cook simply led us to another in a daisy chain of remembered dinners, parties and pot-luck suppers. We were determined to present a cross-section of the town, the weekenders, local residents and businesspeople along with the actresses and artists. We found ourselves in cottage kitchens, log cabins and mansions, on a bench, a bridge, in a monastery and even at the town dump. The people we met welcomed us into their homes and were as interested in sharing their stories and recipes with us as we were in hearing them. Our only regret is that we didn't have the space to include more cooks, or more space to devote to each personality.

Every recipe in this collection has been prepared and tested, and as favorites tried and true they represent a neglected part of Woodstock's lore. Some of these dishes can be prepared in minutes; others may take hours, but all are delicious. And we doubt that you will ever find a more lively collection of food and people anywhere in America!

Joanne Michaels

Mary Barile

November, 1987
Woodstock, NY

3

4

Alf Evers

town historian

"Soybeans are wonderful stuff."

Many readers are familiar with Alf's books of regional history, **The Catskills: From Wilderness to Woodstock** and **Woodstock: History of an American Town,** while others enjoy his children's stories. But few people know that the manna which sustained him during those long years of writing was soybean stew, a dish concocted, in part, due to a meager advance received from his publisher.

"Soybeans are wonderful stuff," according to Alf, a tall, vigorous octogenarian. "Henry Ford was a real soybean enthusiast. They cost 45¢ a pound when I began writing my book on Woodstock in 1972, and now they sell for 55¢ a pound...only a 10¢ increase in 15 years!" There is a sense of vindication when Alf laughingly recalls that "some people told me not to eat soybeans for health reasons. I've eaten my soybean stew almost every day for years and I'm still here... and very vigorous." Alf uses a pressure cooker for food preparation, including the stew, explaining "I pick'em up at yard sales for a dollar. People are afraid they'll explode."

Alf was born in 1905 and moved to Ulster County with his family in 1914, first to a farm in Tillson, then into Woodstock. Alf's father, an architect, specialized in building large country mansions, which went out of style and left him with little work. "My parents became caught up in a back-to-the-land movement, which was popular at the time," he says, explaining how they bought several how-to books before leaving New York City, "so we became farmers of a sort."

As a writer, Alf can empathize with earlier Woodstock artists and musicians who had to live frugally while pursuing the creative life. He recalled how some of them rented living space in a barn for 35¢ a week and stored a bowl and spoon up on a beam above their cot. At milking time they would show up with a box of cornflakes and for 15¢ a week, they had fresh milk with breakfast. About the Maverick, Alf claims that the artists' palettes received more

5

attention than their palates. "Maverick staple foods were lentils and salt pork, then lentils and hot dogs, when they became popular," he says.

Alf's pursuit of regional history has brought him close to people whose memories reach back far enough to recall a past that is mythical to most of us. There was Alf's New Paltz Sunday School teacher, who met Abraham Lincoln in a doorway when they both sought shelter from a rainstorm in Washington, D.C. There was the Pine Hill woman who recalled traveling in her family's wagon to see the first Ulster and Delaware train chug through the Catskills. And there was even the family friend who was a lady-in-waiting at one of the royal courts of Europe.

There is never enough time to listen to Alf's stories, and as we were leaving he noted that "The older you get, the more you seem to remember about the past." Actually, the older Alf gets, the more everyone else learns about the past!

SOYBEAN STEW WITH A HISTORY

While we were talking to Alf, he brought us each a bowl full of this satisfying staple which he prepares nearly every day.

2 cups soybeans
1 8-ounce can tomatoes **OR**
  1 can of tomato soup with 3/4 cup of water **OR**
  1 cup of chopped fresh tomatoes plus 1/2 cup water
1 cup chopped celery
1 medium-sized green pepper, seeded and sliced
2 carrots, peeled and sliced
2 cups mushrooms, sliced
1 tablespoon vinegar
1 teaspoon oregano
1 teaspoon rosemary
salt and pepper to taste
1/4 cup soy sauce, if desired **AND**
"Anything else in the fridge that you think might inspire you."

Soak soybeans in water overnight; drain. Put all of the above ingredients into a pressure cooker. Following manufacturer's directions, cook for approximately 40 minutes. According to Alf, if you re-heat this on top of the stove, add 1/2 cup of grated cheese or hamburger per serving. Or you can put the stew in an ovenproof dish and bake in a woodburning cookstove until surface of the stew is crusty.

ALF'S APPLESAUCE

"I have to watch my sugar intake, so I usually choose a naturally sweet dessert. I like to use red apples, like McIntosh, with the skins on, for my applesauce. I core and seed about six medium-size apples, add one cup of water and simmer them in a pot until they are soft-- don't strain the sauce. Sometimes I add a tablespoon of lemon juice, which cuts the sweetness, and usually I can some of my applesauce and enjoy it year round." Alf suggests serving the applesauce over plain yogurt. He also pointed out that the Jonathan apple originated in Woodstock, and the Esopus Spitzenburgh was another popular local pome. On a related subject, Alf offered a hint for keeping pears, which he learned on the Tillson farm in his boyhood. "Pick the pears before they are ripe. Wrap each one separately in plain paper (or newspaper) and store in a bureau drawer." This should allow them to ripen slowly over several months.

OLD TIME BLACK BIRCH TEA

Sometimes when Alf is out chopping wood, he will come across a black birch branch. "I save the inner bark," he explains. "I grate it and make tea. It tastes just like wintergreen." To make the tea, put 1/2 cup of grated bark in a teapot. Pour very hot (not boiling) water over bark and let steep for 5-7 minutes; boiling water will, in Alf's words, "make the flavor vanish." Strain and serve warm. Black birch was a good substitute for wintergreen, which was more expensive, and had to be distilled before it could be used for medicines and flavorings. A small wintergreen industry grew up around Woodstock; one of the old stills was on Lewis Hollow Road.

7

Susan Carey
True Light Beaver Commune

"We lived in a commune for most of our marriage."

At the age of 48, jeweler Susan Carey told us that 1986 was the first time in almost twenty years that she was living alone with her husband, painter Marty Carey. "We lived in a commune for most of the years of our marriage. Everyone we knew wanted to live communally," she says. "Marty was busy painting and I wanted company while raising the kids," who are now in their twenties and pursuing successful careers in the visual arts.

Susan was talking about her years as a member of the True Light Beaver Commune which flourished in Woodstock from 1969 through the early 1980s. At its peak, there were 17 full-time members -- artists, musicians, writers, hippies, dropouts -- who shared the same philosophy as the Careys. "We came to Woodstock from New Hampshire after living for several years in the East Village," recalls Susan. "We wanted to move to California, but our Volkswagen bus broke down and we had a choice between buying land or a car." The Careys decided to buy land in Woodstock.

Marty and Susan are both natives of Worcester, Massachussetts, like one of their old friends, Abbie Hoffman. The Careys went to the Woodstock Festival, where they sold tie-dyed wall hangings. "We were older hippies, in our late twenties, and we agreed with Abbie that there needed to be some kind of political consciousness at the Festival," said Susan of the muddy, mind-bending celebration.

Like a lot of the Sixties institutions, the unusual name of the True Light Beavers has its own story. Susan was at a shop in the East Village one day and saw basketball shirts with "True Light Beaver" printed on them. The shirts had been made for a Zen basketball team that never picked them up, so Susan bought the lot and the commune had a name.

The True Light Beavers kept busy. They operated a certified school on the premises, The Community Free School. Two books were published: one about their experiences on the commune, **Feast**, and one about their trip to Mexico with the school, **On The Bus**. Susan designed them both.

8

Tasks were shared at the commune. "We drew up an assignment chart that was posted on the refrigerator," explains Susan, adding that cleaning was the least popular activity, but everyone learned to cook. The favorite entree was manicotti, and each chef of the day had his or her own specialties. One member, Chico, "loved soybeans and when it was his turn to cook, the kids hated it," Susan remembers. "The meals were basically vegetarian, although this was as much because we couldn't afford meat at the time as it was due to personal choice."

Susan looks back on those years as rich ones filled with adventures as well as opportunities to learn about herself and others. "It gets to be a very heavy experience when you're sharing the same space with other people. Sharing is a very hard thing to do." But, she adds, "I wouldn't have missed it for the world."

TRUE LIGHT BEAVER PILAF

This recipe came from an Armenian friend of Susan's; it serves 10.

3/4 cup oil
4 1/2 cups fine egg noodles, broken into small pieces
4 1/2 cups uncooked white rice
11 cups boiling water
10-12 bouillon cubes
2 1/2 teaspoons salt
1/2 teaspoon pepper
sour cream, if desired

In a large kettle, brown noodles and rice in oil until noodles are golden brown. Add boiling water and bouillon cubes, stirring until cubes are dissolved. Add salt and pepper, cover the pot and cook at a low boil for 30 minutes. Serve topped with sour cream.

AUTUMN HASH

Fast and easy to make, this dish is colored with the soft yellows and oranges of the autumn harvest.

Oil
1 large onion, cut into slivers
1/2 butternut squash, diced fine
1 medium sweet potato, diced fine
1 small yellow squash, cut into matchsticks
4 cups cooked kasha
tamari

In 1 tablespoon oil, sauté onion until slightly soft; add other vegetables and steam over low heat for 5 minutes with cover on. Mix in kasha, 1 more tablespoon oil and tamari to taste, and press into lightly oiled baking dish. Bake at 350°F for 20 minutes.

COMMUNE CUTLETS

This unusual vegetarian dish can serve as an entree or side dish.

5 cups cooked rice (cook in stock)
6 hard-boiled eggs, mashed
parsley
salt
pepper
chopped peppers or tomatoes
4 eggs
1 cup flour
lemon or lime wedges, if desired

Mix all ingredients together. Form patties and refrigerate till firm. Fry in butter till brown. Serve with lemon or lime wedges.

Michael Lang
organizer, 1969 Woodstock Festival

"I listen to a lot more classical music now."

The weekend of August 15, 1969, has come to symbolize the spirit of the decade-- and a generation. The Woodstock Music and Art Fair: An Aquarian Exposition, as the event was originally named, actually took place in Bethel, New York, approximately 50 miles from the town of Woodstock. The festival was held in Sullivan County, since the town of Woodstock was ruled out as too small to accommodate the expected turnout. Looking back at that time, Michael, now in his early forties, says, "I had a <u>great</u> time. Being able to put such an event together with all its complicated aspects was challenging and fun."

Michael has lived in Woodstock since 1968 and is now president of New York-based Better Music Incorporated, a management and production company which he founded and whose clients include Joe Cocker, Rickie Lee Jones and Mick Ronson. "Since the Sixties, my taste in music has expanded, and I listen to a lot more classical music now," says Michael about the evolution of his musical taste. He also feels that the actual music of the Eighties isn't so different in quality from the music of the Sixites, but it is "less socially concerned, less exciting. There's none of that pioneering spirit."

When the subject turns to food, Michael explains that he travels a great deal and doesn't have much time to cook. Since the days of the Festival, however, his culinary tastes have also broadened. "I eat all kinds of unusual foods now," he says, going on to mention Thai and Greek cuisines as a couple of his favorites. Maybe Michael will stage a festival for aging baby-boomers in the year 2000. And maybe this time, the festival will take place in Woodstock!

AQUARIAN BREAKFAST

   This late morning meal is not your typical All-American breakfast, but then, Michael is not your typical breakfast eater.

   "I slice tomatoes and some goat cheese, pour on some olive oil and wine vinegar, then add salt and pepper. Usually, I have crackers and strong tea with it."

Sally Grossman
Bearsville Sound Studio

"Albert still sends me little gifts."

Sally's late husband, Albert Grossman, was the founder of Bearsville Sound Studio and represented some of the top Sixties musical talent, including Peter, Paul and Mary, Janis Joplin, and Bob Dylan. Sally, a native of Queens, now runs the business, which is well-known for its quality recording work and is used by rock artists like Chrissie Hynde and Til Tuesday.

Sally's way to Woodstock was as roundabout as many others: "I met Albert when I was waitressing at **The Cafe Wha** and **The Bitter End** in Greenwich Village," she laughs as she recalls her "escape" from Queens. "Peter Yarrow owned a cabin in Woodstock, and would bring Dylan up from New York City to visit, so we were familiar with the area. And after Milton Glaser told us about this wonderful house that was on the market, we bought it and moved here in 1964." Sally's wedding was as typical of Woodstock as anything else in the Sixties. "We were married by a Justice of the Peace in Bearsville, and after that, it was easier for me to charge things under Albert's name at the hardware store," she laughs.

Albert's influence is still pervasive in the recording world, and the youthful Sally finds it funny when younger musicians refer to her and Albert's work as "legendary." Although much of her time is spent managing the studio, Sally also has a home near Oaxaca in Mexico, where she is recognized as a specialist in Southern Mexican textiles, and where "you can walk out in the backyard and pick up artifacts and pottery pieces after nearly every rainfall." As we leave, Sally gives us a handful of freshly harvested chestnuts, pleased that "Albert still sends me little gifts. He planted these trees. And now I'm enjoying them."

WILD BEARSVILLE RICE

Sally has served this popular dish, a favorite of Albert's, to vegetarians, rock groups and wedding parties. "I always made huge amounts of it, and when we took it somewhere, people would come up to Albert and say, 'You're such a great cook! ' That was our secret, something we always laughed about."

1 cup wild rice
2 cups water
2 garlic cloves
mayonnaise (homemade is best, but you can substitute prepared mayonnaise)
3 medium tomatoes, peeled, seeded and coarsely chopped (to make peeling easier, plunge tomatoes into boiling water for a few seconds; the skins should slip right off)
tomato juice (reserve from tomatoes or substitute 1/8 cup canned juice)
thyme, to taste
rosemary, to taste
salad greens, if desired

Place the rice in a large saucepan with water. Bring the water to a boil, then reduce the heat, cover and simmer rice until the water is absorbed. In the meantime, use a garlic press and squeeze the garlic cloves into the mayonnaise; stir in the tomatoes, juice, thyme and rosemary. When the rice has cooled, toss together with mayonnaise mixture. Serve chilled, on a bed of greens.

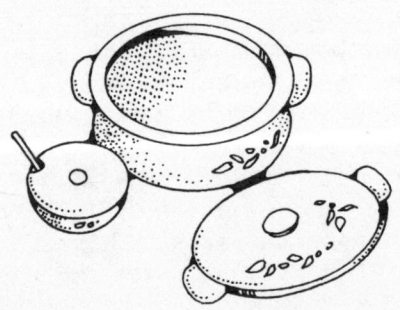

Albert Hoffman

proprietor, Twin Gables Guest House

"We're fifty years behind the times."

"The Hoffman family bought Twin Gables in 1940 and has been operating the guest home, the last of its kind in Woodstock, ever since," Albert explained as he showed us into the kitchen of Twin Gables, a high-ceilinged room filled with memories of old Woodstock.

Albert opened an oak sideboard and pulled out a large, leatherbound guest register from 1905, when the building was known as the Twin Gables Tea House. Visitors to Woodstock enjoyed stopping there for a refreshing drink and a slice of cake, served on the terrace at colorful umbrella shaded tables. In the 1920s and 30s, Twin Gables was "the center of sociability in the town," according to Albert, and it wasn't uncommon for guests to run up large tabs. One of the account books showed bills that ran on for six months at a time when the cost of a night's lodging was $3.

GRANDMOTHER'S POUND CAKE

Tea drinkers at Twin Gables enjoyed this cake while having their afternoon repast on the terrace more than 80 years ago.

1 cup butter
1 2/3 cups sugar
5 eggs
2 cups flour
2 teaspoons vanilla

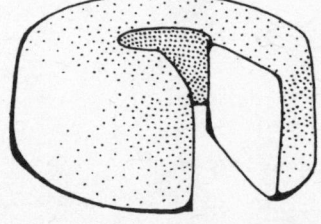

Preheat oven to 325°F. Work butter until creamy and add sugar gradually. Mix in the eggs, one at a time, beating vigorously between the addition of each egg. When the mixture is of a creamy consistency, fold in the flour, add vanilla and turn into a buttered and floured pound cake pan or Bundt pan. Bake one hour or until a toothpick inserted in center of cake comes out clean.

25

Barbara Shultis Forno
homemaker

"I remember going to ice-skating parties on Yankeetown Pond."

The Shultis family has been in Woodstock since the 18th century, with many of those years spent on their farm in Wittenberg. Barbara and her husband, Big Joe, owner of the Colonial Pharmacy, still live on land owned by Barbara's grandfather.

Barbara recalls a rural Woodstock with echoes of a 19th century Currier and Ives print. "I remember going to ice-skating parties on Yankeetown Pond," she says. "We would build a big bonfire on the ice which was so thick it wouldn't burn through. It was beautiful, with the moonlight reflecting off the snow and ice on a winter's evening."

One of Barbara's hobbies is collecting old cookbooks, and a few date to the early years of Woodstock's art colony, when cooks, including Jane Whitehead, offered their favorite recipes. Although Barbara has a cookbook from 1938, she notes that there was an even earlier one. "My aunt, who is 101 years old, told me about the book, and I'm still trying to track it down," she laughs. Anyone out there with a copy?

SHULTIS SHORTCAKE

These ultra-rich, buttery biscuits "don't raise up much" because of the shortening in them, but we bet you won't count calories when they're on the table. The best way to serve them according to Barbara: "Split'em with a fork, not a knife, and top with fresh wild strawberries and soft whipped cream. That's how we used to eat them during summers in Woodstock when I was growing up!"

2 cups flour
2 teaspoons baking powder
1/2 teaspoon salt

16

2 tablespoons sugar
1/2 cup butter
1/2 cup milk
1/2 cup water

   Preheat oven to 400°F. Sift together the flour, baking powder, salt and sugar. Cut in the butter with a pastry blender or two knives. Mix the milk and water together, then add liquid a few tablespoons at a time to flour mixture, stirring only enough to moisten (do not overmix). You may not need all the liquid, since the dough should be sticky, not runny. Drop by rounded tablespoons onto an ungreased cookie sheet and bake for 10-15 minutes, or until golden. Serve warm.

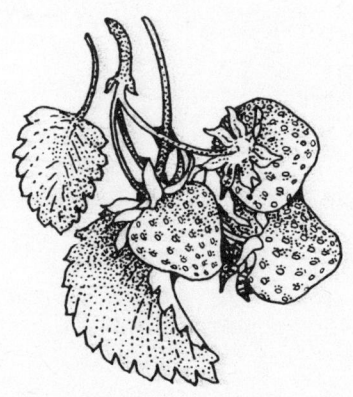

Anne & Howard Koch

screenwriters

"The Humphrey Bogart role almost went to Ronald Reagan."

Although many Woodstock residents know that Howard was a scriptwriter for both the film **Casablanca** and the radio classic **War of the Worlds,** few realize that he was raised in Kingston, "a conservative, Republican town." No wonder the aspiring playwright traveled to "wild" Woodstock by bus. Even then, it was the perfect place for a teenager.

But Howard didn't become involved with Woodstock's cultural scene until he was a student at Bard College, across the river in Annandale. One summer, a theater company under the direction of Hervey White found itself in a common artistic condition: broke. Unable to pay the royalties a "name" playwright would command, White was desperate for material until he remembered that a local lad had written a play. **The Philosopher** by Howard Koch told the story of a college student trying to convince his family that his way of thinking was best. White contacted Howard, who agreed to the staging of the comedy/satire. And in the great tradition of the American stage, a producer saw the play and brought it to Broadway under the title **He Went to College.** The kid who went to Woodstock to see the artists was now a glimmer on the Great White Way.

Howard spent several years working in Hollywood, but when he and his wife Anne were blacklisted during the McCarthy era, they looked for a place of refuge from the insanity that was suffocating America. They found peace in Woodstock. And for the last 30 years, when Howard and Anne aren't back in California, they live in a gracious home on the banks of the Sawkill.

Of course, you can't talk to Howard without mentioning **Casablanca,** and so we asked him about the making of the movie. "Part of the script was written on the set," says Howard, "the worst way to make a movie, and there were two different endings written, one happy and one political.

18

Ingrid Bergman was baffled about how to play the romantic scenes without knowing who her love interest was going to be." And here's one for trivia buffs: the Humphrey Bogart role almost went to Ronald Reagan! With these near misses in mind, Howard says in retrospect, "It was mystical that the movie all came together. **Casablanca** belongs to the people; that's the best thing about it."

FIRST ACT FRENCH TOAST (Script by Howard Koch)

This family recipe arose out of desperation years ago, when the Kochs discovered that their young son would get cranky if there were too many people in the kitchen. So sensible Anne headed back to bed, and Howard was left to create a new production on his own.

"Put three eggs (for two people) in a pure silver bowl (Howard was very adamant on this point) and beat the hell out of them with a fork. Add two cups of fresh cow's milk from cows milked that morning and beat again." (On the subject of milk, the following Anne and Howard debate occurred: "It is only one cup of milk." "I still think it is two." "Howard, that's half a quart!" "I'm beginning to wonder whose recipe this is anyway." Please note, they did settle on one cup.)

"Add a dash of Worcestershire sauce and a little salt. Put the bread in the bowl to soak and let the mixture stand for 10 minutes. Meanwhile, heat a small pan with a good hunk of butter. When the butter melts, add bread slices to the skillet." (Here, another controversy arose over whether to add the remaining contents of the silver bowl to the pan or to make another helping. Howard's solution: Dump it all in and hope for the best.)

"Serve the French Toast on a silver dish. Pour very pure maple syrup over each piece, and complete the breakfast with freshly ground Columbian coffee and a grapefruit, but make sure all the little segments are cut well."

End of scene. Fade out.

ANNE'S BROILED PEPPERS RELLENOS

Howard says of his wife and editor, "she is keen on what is right in life as well as in films." A fine screenwriter in her own right, Anne scripted some of the early **Robin Hood** films. Her incredulous reaction upon hearing a request for a recipe from Howard was, "Howard cook?!" Howard did not disagree, claiming that Anne was the family chef. So here is Howard's favorite recipe from his favorite editor.

2 green peppers, quartered lengthwise and seeded
1/2 cup shredded cheddar cheese
1/4 cup mayonnaise
2 tablespoons sliced green onion
2 egg whites, stiffly beaten

If using fresh peppers, cook in boiling water three minutes or until tender; drain. Place on a cold broiler rack. Stir together half the cheese, mayonnaise and green onion. Fold in egg whites. Spoon mixture into peppers, spreading to cover the edges. Sprinkle with remaining cheese. Broil about 5" away from heat for 5 minutes or until cheese is melted. Makes six to eight appetizers.

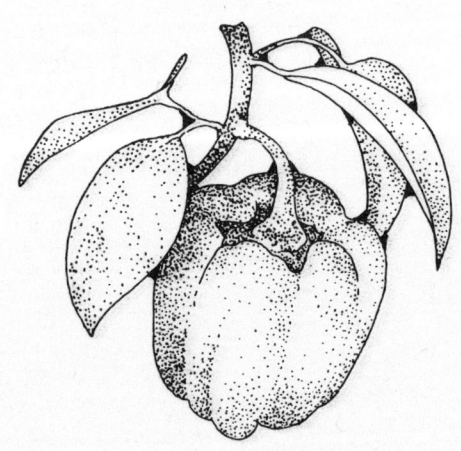

Jane & Happy Traum
Homespun Tapes

"It was just a bunch of Woodstock people getting together."

Happy's albums, including the 1972 folk classic **Mud Acres**, have featured Woodstock musicians past and present: John Herald, Maria Muldaur, John Sebastian, Paul Butterfield, and Eric Kaz. But even with all the talent (and personalities), "it was just a bunch of Woodstock people getting together like we were at a party," recalls Happy, who also has solo and other albums recorded with his brother, musician Artie Traum.

Today, Happy and his wife, Jane, are the founders and owners of a unique music production company, **Homespun Tapes**, which has been in business since 1967. The Traums produce audio instructional tapes and videos for musicians. "We started putting tapes together when Happy was touring and needed to leave instructional sessions for his students," explains Jane. The Traums added to the tape production using a core of Woodstock musicians, and have since expanded and offer more than 300 types of lessons on a variety of instruments. The tapes are sold worldwide and include gospel, country, jazz, folk and bluegrass music. And about Happy's name. "I've always been called Happy, ever since I was a kid," he laughs, "but that's not the name on my birth certificate." The real one's a secret.

HOMESPUN CABBAGE & APPLES

Jane enjoys making this dish for holiday parties, noting that it's really convenient since the longer it stays in the pot, the more mellow the flavors become. You can vary the dish by using red cabbage, omitting the sausage, curry, turmeric and sprinkling with poppy seeds before serving.

21

1 large white cabbage, shredded
4 medium onions, peeled and sliced
vegetable oil or butter
1 or 2 medium apples, cored and sectioned (leave the skin
   on)
1/4 cup water
1 cup apple cider
salt and pepper
curry powder
turmeric
2 chicken sausages, boiled and sliced

       Shred cabbage and saute with onions in oil; stir
in apples. Add water, cider, salt and pepper, curry and turmeric
to taste. Bring mixture to a boil and reduce heat to a simmer.
For the last five minutes of cooking, add sausage slices.
Remove from heat and let sit for one hour before serving.
Serve cold or warm.

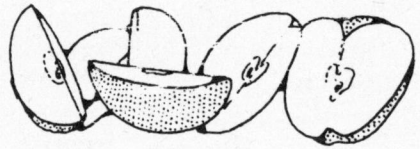

Manette Van Hamel

artist

"By the time Martine was 11, we were told she had a very rare talent."

Although the Maverick Concerts are well known as the oldest continuously operating chamber music series in the United States, there aren't many people in Woodstock who remember the annual pig roasts thrown by Hervey White at the Maverick.

Manette does-- she lived on the Maverick property in 1920 with her mother, a pianist, and father, a writer and foreign correspondent. "I was only six, but my brother and I were allowed to stay up late and dance into the night," she recalls, referring to the festive event. "One year, we were scared to death, because we heard that the Ku Klux Klan was going to show up at the Maverick, but the party went on as usual," and the Klan stayed away. The Maverick was a wonderful place to grow up, and Manette can still reel off the names of French, Swedish, Russian and Dutch musicians and writers who lived in this unusual community.

Dutch by birth, Manette has traveled and lived around the world-- first with her parents and then with her husband, a diplomat, and their three children. The Van Hamels finally re-settled in Woodstock in the 1950s, and Manette's husband, now retired, is a craftsman who makes violins and violas.

But living in places like South America, Canada and Indonesia also created some unusual problems for the family. "By the time our daughter, Martine, was eleven, we were told by a renowned Russian ballet instructor that she had a very rare talent," says Manette. "Part of our challenge was to find first-rate instruction in cities such as Toronto and Caracas, but fortunately, both cities had dance companies and schools that Martine could attend." The result was worth the effort, of course: Martine became a prima ballerina with the New York City Ballet under the direction of George Balanchine.

23

Manette herself is a talented artist and jewelry designer. When poor eyesight made jewelry work difficult, she turned to painting full time. Describing what motivated her to display the paintings outdoors, in the largest gallery of all, Manette laughs: "too many paintings, not enough walls." The large canvases, full of bright colors, geometric forms, and sculptural in feel, change in their natural setting from season to season. Each canvas is mounted so that both sides are visible, allowing a viewer to enjoy two different landscapes by taking only a few steps. Add to this the sound of a nearby brook, and you can begin to appreciate the innovative talent of Manette, a woman who makes her surroundings part of her art.

GADO GADO VAN HAMEL

After living in Indonesia for three years, Manette mastered some of the native cuisine. Over thirty years later, she was able to recall this recipe, a particular favorite of Martine's.

4 carrots, scraped and julienned
2 cups shredded raw cabbage
2 cups chopped celery
1 cup snow peas
1 cup bean sprouts
1 bunch (approximately 6) scallions, sliced
4 hardboiled eggs, sliced
grated coconut, if desired
prepared white rice
Pretty Perfect Peanut Sauce (see recipe)

In a vegetable steamer (or medium-size saucepan), steam vegetables for two to three minutes; they should remain crisp. Drain and arrange on a large platter and place egg slices around the edge of platter. Chill for two hours before serving. Pour Pretty Perfect Peanut Sauce over vegetables and garnish with grated coconut, if desired. Serve with white rice.

SIMPLY SATÉ

2 pounds pork loin, trimmed and cut into cubes
2 cups soy sauce
1/2 cup lemon juice
1/2 cup chopped onions
1 tablespoon finely chopped fresh ginger
4 cloves garlic, finely chopped
salt and pepper, to taste
hot sauce (Sambol), to taste

Place cubes of pork on short skewers (12" is a good length.) Mix remaining ingredients together and place in a tall, deep container, so that skewers can stand upright; allow to marinate for 2 hours. Remove skewers and reserve marinade. Barbecue or grill pork for 15 minutes over hot fire or until pork is thoroughly cooked. Serve with Gado Gado and Peanut Sauce.

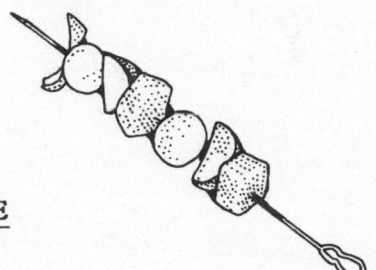

PRETTY PERFECT PEANUT SAUCE

1/2 cup peanut butter
1 cup of marinade from Saté (recipe above)

In a small sauce pan, stir peanut butter into marinade. Bring mixture to a boil and remove from heat immediately. If mixture has thickened so that it cannot be easily poured, add 1/4 cup warm water and return to heat. Warm mixture; do not boil. Serve over Gado Gado or as a dip for Saté.

Mary Orser

astrologer

"I'm eating more unprocessed blue-green algae."

Just off Camelot Road, where the karmas of Byrdcliffe and Dylan meet, sits a timber-frame house filled with light, rock crystals and zodiacs, home to astrologer Mary Orser, and Rasta, her cat.

A resident of Woodstock for more than thirty years, Texas-born Mary holds advanced degrees in both journalism and psychology, an unusual background for a highly respected caster of nativities. But then, Mary doesn't hold much with the usual in life. She came to Woodstock while searching for a mountain place and for a while worked as a secretary to the president of Rotron. During a particularly rough period in her life, she consulted an astrologer for a hint of the future. After doing a reading he told Mary that with her chart (Capricorn with Capricorn rising) she might be better off studying astrology than just listening. Today, Mary has four books on the subject to her credit, and she offers readings and classes throughout the Hudson Valley.

A "new age" astrologer who uses a computer to draw charts, Mary compares the art of astrology to "reading the score of cosmic music." She explains, "Energy is neither good nor bad, it depends upon how it is used. I don't presume to tell people what decisions to make about their lives, I only tell them the type of personal 'weather' they may be facing."

As to reading the future without a chart, Mary is as prone to problems as the rest of the world. The winter before the Woodstock Festival, organizer Michael Lang was at a party at her home. "He announced that the next summer we were going to have the biggest festival ever," Mary recalled. "He looked so young, at the time I didn't believe him. I really didn't think he could pull something like that off so I replied 'How nice, Michael!'"

Astrology aside, for the last forty years, Mary has been a vegetarian. And since 1985, she has maintained a raw foods diet that precludes eggs, cheese and cooked foods. Her belief that vital enzymes in food are destroyed even at moderate temperatures has led her to develop a diet of juices, vegetables, fruits, and salads that are garden grown or foraged in season.

Mary notes that today's vegetarians have it a little easier with food processors and blenders, but there are times when travel or the winter months can make it difficult to come up with something interesting. Sometimes she uses a food dehydrator to prepare dried fruits and her own herb-flavored onion crackers. When asked about variety in such a diet, Mary says, "I'm eating more unprocessed blue-green algae lately, which I order from Oregon." Even raw food addicts have their own nouvelle cuisine.

CAPRICORN RISING GAZPACHO

juice of two lemons
1/2 cup carrot juice
2 cups chopped raw tomatoes
1/2 teaspoon oregano
1/2 teaspoon kelp
2 medium cloves garlic
1 tablespoon olive oil
grated carrot & chopped fresh parsley, if desired
chopped cucumber & sliced scallions, if desired

Put first seven ingredients into a blender and blend until smooth. Gazpacho may be served topped with grated carrot, fresh parsley, chopped cucumber or scallions.

HEAVENLY NUT LOAF

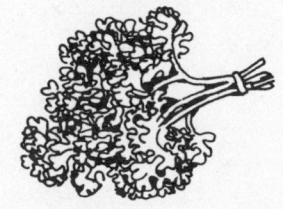

1/2 cup ground almonds
1/2 cup ground cashews
2 cups finely grated carrots
1/2 cup finely chopped onion
1/2 cup finely chopped parsley
2 tablespoons safflower or sunflower oil
favorite seasonings to taste

In a large bowl, thoroughly mix all ingredients. Shape into a loaf by pressing mixture into a small loaf pan. Chill for three hours, if desired. Slice and serve.

Bill Newgold

promoter

"Alfred Knopf didn't believe in the future of radio."

Bill Newgold's relationship with Woodstock began in 1916 when his family purchased the Overlook Mountain House. As a youth, he spent summers working in the hotel business, and later, he helped his father build the Colony Hotel, a unique brick building on Rock City Road constructed from local materials and decorated with the work of area artists such as Woodstock blacksmith Henry Peper.

Although a full-time resident of Woodstock for many years, Bill spent part of his career working as a publicist for publisher Alfred Knopf, where he dealt with writers H.L. Mencken, George Jean Nathan, Willa Cather, Sherwood Anderson and others. At the time, Bill was approached by Mencken, who edited **The Mercury** magazine, to host a series of radio broadcasts about writers. "The manager at NBC radio didn't believe I could write a fifteen minute script, even though Mencken had written a letter of recommendation in which he said I was the best young critic in the country next to himself," laughs Bill. "What he forgot to tell NBC, was that I was the only young critic 'next' to himself-- we shared office space at Knopf and our desks were next to each other." Bill got the job, but only after producing two scripts. The first one had been torn apart and rewritten by Mencken and friends; "a brilliant gem" was the result, but Bill finally was able to write his own and have it accepted. The radio show was a success and Bill was forced to leave his job at Knopf: Alfred Knopf didn't believe in the future of radio and told Bill he was wasting his time. Bill decided to take a chance.

Over the years, Bill learned to cook from various chefs employed by his family. These experiences, coupled with Bill's own sense of taste, led him to develop a distinctive philosophy of gourmet cooking. "Knowing when and how to use ten key ingredients can put you right up there with the best chefs in New York, New Orleans, San Francisco,

Paris and Rome," he believes. The ingredients? "Cheese, butter, mushrooms, wine, garlic, nuts, herbs and spices, fruits, cream and coloring."

Bill has never acquired a taste for frozen food. "If I were to be deprived of all my crusades except one," he says, "the one I would keep would be the League in Opposition to Serving Frozen TV Dinners to Human Beings." He does feel, however, that there must be some use for TV dinners in the world-- other than eating them.

COLONY HORS D'OEUVRES PLATTER

Bill prepares appetizers to please visitors at the Woodstock Colony Arts Center, which is housed in the old Colony Hotel. The following tidbits are "just about foolproof" according to Bill, and preparation time for all three hors d'oeuvres is approximately 90 minutes; add 30 minutes for cooking. This recipe is for one of his favorite platters which always goes over well, with critics, artists, viewers, anyone.

Miniature Meatballs

Preheat oven to 350°F. Grease a 9"-square pan with olive oil; set aside. Assemble the following ingredients in an 8 ounce measuring cup:

    2 tablespoons parsley flakes
    2 tablespoons seasoned bread crumbs
    4 tablespoons grated parmesan cheese
    1 tablespoon ground pepper
    1 tablespoon salt
    1 tablespoon minced garlic
    1 teaspoon oregano

Fill rest of cup to top with dried onion flakes. Crumble a pound of ground round into a bowl; stir in 8 ounces of burgundy and then thoroughly mix in spices. Form meat mixture into approximately 16 meatballs; set aside. In a separate bowl, mix together an 8 ounce can of tomato sauce, 4 ounces (one-half can) of water, and one or two teaspoons of Worcestershire sauce. Place the meatballs in the pan, carefully pour the tomato sauce mixture over them and bake for 30 minutes; baste the meatballs every 10 minutes.

Stuffed Mushrooms

Preheat oven to 350°F; grease a 9"-square baking pan with olive oil and set aside. Wash and stem 1 pound of large, short-stemmed mushrooms (approximately 16 mushrooms.) Slice the stems lengthwise and save for the Chicken Livers (see recipe.) Place the mushroom caps upside down in the pan, and fill each stem cavity with olive oil; this will soak into the mushrooms. Next, in an 8 ounce measuring cup mix together:

> 1 teaspoon grated pepper
> 1/4 cup seasoned bread crumbs
> 1/2 cup grated parmesan cheese
> 2 tablespoons minced garlic
> 1 tablespoon garlic powder
> 1 tablespoon oregano
> 4 tablespoons parsley flakes
> 2 generous pinches dried onion flakes

Fill mushroom caps with herb mixture; press gently into caps. Moisten the tops of the mixture with olive oil. Bake for 15 minutes, then re-moisten the herb mixture with olive oil and bake for 15 minutes; serve warm.

Sautéed Chicken Livers

Preheat oven to 350°F. Wash 1 pound fresh chicken livers (not frozen) in cold water; dry on paper towels. Trim away gristle or fat and cut livers into bite-sized portions. In a small bowl, mix together livers, mushroom stems (use leftover stems from previous recipe or add 1/2 cup sliced mushrooms) and dried onion flakes to taste. Melt 1/4 pound butter or margarine in 9" square baking pan; spread evenly over pan. Spoon livers into pan and bake for 10 minutes; turn with spatula, add a cup of white wine and allow to simmer for 20 minutes or until the livers are cooked thoroughly.

30

Sylvia Miles

actress

"It's what I call comedy cooking. "

Two-time Academy Award nominee, internationally acclaimed actress and Greenwich Village native, Sylvia has lived in Woodstock since 1982. Her television and stage credits are impressive, and her film credits include such classics as Andy Warhol's **Heat, Midnight Cowboy, Farewell My Lovely, Evil Under the Sun,** and more recently, **Wall Street** and **Throwback.**

Sophisticated and down-to-earth, brusque and warm, feisty and funny: these only begin to describe Sylvia, who, within ten minutes, makes you feel like you've known her forever. Her home, whose interior she designed, reflects her personality and her career, from the **Heat** poster to the African drums, the hide-covered chairs and her childhood bed. "I was looking for something funky and elegant in a house," she says. "I didn't want to be like the people who come up from the city and gentrify the woods."

Sylvia's stove looks brand–new, even after six years of ownership, and the refrigerator holds only a few cans of soda. "I'm a working actress, and I never know where I'm going to be. I have to keep supplies on hand for fast meals. Everything has to be quick in my house-- quick iced tea, quick lemonade," she continues, taking out a colorful array of cans from the cupboard. "When someone visits, I always serve a combination of canned or gourmet convenience foods. I make things quickly by adding on and mixing. I can take an instant noodle dish, throw in some canned chicken and have a meal. It's what I call comedy cooking. Look at this," she says, displaying two cans for our examination. "This is brie in a tin, and a can of shrimp for my instant shrimp cocktail. I've learned to carry cans with me since I'm on location a lot and you never know what you're going to get in some parts of Africa and India."

A favorite breakfast of Sylvia's is matzoh topped with a sliced banana, and "one of the best things in the world is Dinty Moore's Beef Stew," she claims, at least compared to some of the stews served at international dining spots. When we met with Sylvia, she had just returned from Israel, where she played the part of the Red Fairy in the film **Sleeping Beauty**, and a few days later she was to report to New York City to begin working on **Crossing Delancey Street.** "I'm at the peak of my career now," she says, with a smile of satisfaction. "I can get the best roles now, and I have to go wherever they take me." Canned food and all.

SYLVIA'S FAST CHICKEN

"Go get frozen chicken parts-- this recipe is great, you don't have to do anything. Don't defrost the chicken. Get a big pan and put the chicken in with some dried onions, canned mushrooms-- those button mushrooms with the butter sauce-- and some wine. Cover and cook for for about 25 minutes. You don't even have to make a trip to the Grand Union to buy onions. And you don't have to clean any mushrooms."

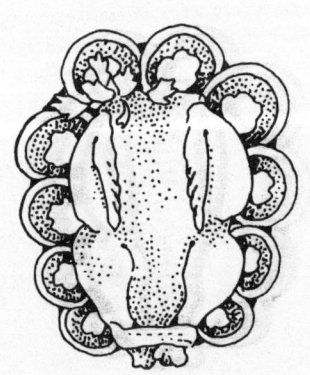

The Rainbow Man & Lady Rainbow

a colorful couple

"I add my peach wine to beans."

The Rainbow Store and owners Thom and Mary Klika, were for years a favorite part of Woodstock's scene. Thom, best known as the exuberant "Rainbow Man," could occasionally be seen greeting customers decked out in rainbow top hat, a rainbow colored wig, and with an earring and tooth decal to match. But the rainbows, as much as they belonged to Woodstock, started elsewhere.

Thom was living on Cape Cod in the Sixties, working as an artist and producing 2-inch miniature watercolor paintings. "The rainbow became one of the symbols," Tom remembers, explaining how he was turning out 500-1,000 of them a day. "I was passing them out to hitchhikers and putting them in mailboxes. But I didn't know I was the Rainbow Man until a friend in California sent me a card with my artwork reproduced on it, and on the back was written, 'by the Rainbow Man.' The stuff had traveled across the country and came back to me. Then I decided to adopt the name."

Thom's wife, Mary, a/k/a Lady Rainbow, was one of the few people we met who had actually been at the 1969 Woodstock Festival. She had gone with a girlfriend to sell mandala t-shirts. "We ended up having to give the shirts away-- the beginning of the non-profit generation," she laughs. Of the food situation at the fest, Mary recalls, "We lived on brown rice, beans and onions, with a lot of soy. I bought some corn from a local farmer; he considered it feed corn...We didn't even think about the butter!" She smiles as she says, "We lived on love, I tell you--and ether. The air around us is what sustained us." One of the most unusual people Mary encountered at the Festival was a nun from Ireland who slept under their van. "She had come to Woodstock to find out more about American youth," Mary explained, "and she certainly did!"

The Klikas enjoy cooking and both have their specialties. Thom is into barbecuing, "especially marinated fish and corn on the cob." Mary likes to prepare chicken, and beans. For years she has been making her own wines and uses them for cooking. "I add peach wine to my beans, and sometimes I sauté chicken in it," she says, suggesting that you try elderflower wine for cooking fish.

When asked what they would bring to a pot luck supper, the Klikas agree on a casserole. And Mary adds, "When we go to a party where there are going to be lots of vegetarians, we bring a chicken dish and I've noticed that it disappears quickly. There are always going to be people there who are absolutely desperate for some meat!"

FULL SPECTRUM MARBLE CAKE

This colorful cake is dazzling, but simple. Just follow the directions for placing the colors and the colors will mix themselves.

1 package white cake mix
red, yellow and blue food colors

Prepare the cake mix according to directions, or use your favorite white cake recipe. Set aside three 1/2 cup portions of batter and pour the remainder into a 9" by 11" pan that has been greased and floured. To each of the 1/2 cup portions, add 3-5 drops of one food color so that you have 1/2 cup each of red, blue and yellow. Next, spoon 1/4 cup of each of the colored batters into the cake mix in the baking pan, making a half circle. Then, repeat the procedure with the remaining 1/4 cup portions (you should have a full circle of red, blue, yellow, red, blue, yellow.) Using a knife, blend the colors together with swirling strokes, so that the colors will touch and mix into the colors of the rainbow. Bake the cake as directed. Frost with your favorite frosting or dust with confectioner's sugar.

CATSKILL CACCIATORE

Mary tells us, "Sweet marjoram and thyme grow wild in this area of the Catskills, by the roadside and in open meadows. Both have purple flowers and can be used fresh but of course, you may substitute the dried variety."

2 whole chicken breasts with skin, cut up into 8 pieces
1 onion, finely chopped
1 large garlic clove, cut into small pieces
2 tablespoons olive oil
1 tablespoon fresh chopped thyme
1 tablespoon fresh chopped marjoram
12 mushrooms, cut into quarters
2 green peppers, cut into 1" pieces
2 onions, cut into quarters
one-pound can whole tomatoes, juice drained and reserved
freshly ground pepper to taste

Put the chicken in a bowl, adding the chopped onion, garlic, oil, thyme, and marjoram; mix well and let stand one hour. Place chicken and herb mixture in an electric frying pan or large skillet. Brown the chicken, reduce heat, add a little water and simmer for 15 minutes. Remove chicken from the pan but leave all remaining liquid. Add a little extra olive oil, if necessary, and cook the mushrooms, green peppers, onions and tomatoes in the liquid approximately 15 minutes or until vegetables and seasonings begin to get tender. Add the chicken and juice from the tomatoes and simmer for one hour. Top with freshly ground pepper before serving.

RAINBOW PARTY PUNCH

If you don't see rainbows after a couple of glasses of this punch, then you're probably color blind. Thom notes that you should "be prepared to make this several times during the course of the evening. And don't forget to provide straws so you can get to the last drops."

1 bottle champagne
1 bottle ginger ale
1/2 cup bourbon
1/4 cup Triple Sec
1 pint rainbow or raspberry sherbet

Chill champagne and ginger ale. Spoon sherbet into a punch bowl, and pour champagne, ginger ale, bourbon and Triple Sec into the bowl. Serve immediately.

Judith Crist
film critic

"We have a split personality in our family."

Judith speaks enthusiastically about her "three major daily occupations": writing for **TV Guide,** acting as arts critic for television and serving as adjunct professor at the Columbia Graduate School of Journalism (her alma mater.) A native New Yorker, Judith, and husband Bill, have been residents of Woodstock since 1972. "We have a split personality in our family," she says, explaining that Bill, now retired, lives in Woodstock all week, while she is there Friday through Monday. Judith hums a few bars of a song friends made up about her domestic arrangements to the tune of "Side by Side." "Oh, the Crists have quite a wifestyle...but they manage to meet, three days a week, side by side." But there are some advantages to this lifestyle, as Judith explains. "I go back to Manhattan on Mondays with loads of canned goods and food from the Grand Union because they are half the price of what I pay on the Upper West Side, which has become so chi-chi!"

Crist likes the "total relaxation" of Woodstock. "The town is laid back in the very best sense," she says. "I can wear the clothes I like without ever being worried about the clothes I'm being seen in." There is a "spaciness" about Woodstock, she feels, in every sense of the word. "There are plenty of spaced-out loonies, but also, physically, there is more space than in the average town."

Judith feels that people are still drawn to Woodstock in part by its reputation as an arts colony and hippie paradise. "It's neither," she maintains. "There is no arts colony anymore and the hippies have all grown old and successful!"

On weekends, the Crists enjoy relaxing and socializing. "Woodstock weekends, for me, involve lots of good friends, good cooks among them, who like to congregate in a big kitchen and carry the burden of the meals to come," says Judith. "When the burden, whole or in part, falls on me, I like to rely on quick and easy favorites."

36

CRIST HOUSE CHICKEN

This is a "put in the oven and forget" dish, according to Judith, and allows for late arrivals and/or an extended cocktail hour. She suggests serving with a salad and garlic bread.

"Fill the bottom of a roasting pan with the chicken needed for the dinner-- parts, breasts, in portions or pieces, and bake as is for a half hour at 350°F. I think it is juicier if left on the bone, but fancy cooks will want to de-bone it. Cover the bottom of the pan with the semi-cooked chicken in a single layer, seasoning top and bottom with salt, paprika, garlic, thyme or whatever is your choice. Take one can of cream of chicken, mushroom or celery soup and spread it, undiluted, over the chicken. Add a layer of sliced swiss cheese or mozzarella and a layer of defrosted (or parboiled, if fresh) broccoli or asparagus. If, by the way, you've used cream of mushroom soup, add mushrooms (preferably fresh but canned if need be) in between the chicken pieces before adding the first layer of cheese. Cover it all with more slices of cheese. Rinse out the soup can with half a can or a little more of dry vermouth and pour it over the mixture. Bake at 325°F for an hour, checking halfway to see that there's enough moisture. If there isn't-- swoosh some more vermouth over it all. You can lower the heat after an hour and keep it going until you're ready to eat."

RAVE REVIEW AMBROSIA

Simple and fast, this dessert is elegant as well.

"To a pint of sour cream add a teaspoon of vanilla and half a cup of brown sugar (or adjust the amount of brown sugar to your taste). Mix well and pour over two and a half pounds of washed (and drained dry) seedless green grapes. Seedless reds are okay for color but the tartness of the greens is needed. Mix well and refrigerate until ready to serve."

FRUIT SALAD FOR THE NON-AA CROWD

"Add 4 ounces of bourbon to 8 ounces of honey and stir; the consistency should be on the runny side but not watery. Pour it into a bowl of cut-up fresh fruit (minus bananas, which can be added at the last minute if you insist on bananas in fruit salad) and refrigerate, stirring a couple of times, until ready to serve. Peaches, plums, cantaloupe, honeydew-- anything and whatever with color to please you. Let the cookies you serve it with supply the sweet. This is a non-sugary dessert for the educated palate."

APPLE TORTE FROM TOBY SUTTON'S FRIEND

Judith offers this apple torte, which she received from a Woodstock friend, Toby Sutton, with the notation "How can it not be good?"

1/4 cup softened butter
1 stick sweet butter, chilled until firm
1 1/8 cups flour
3 heaping tablespoons sugar, if desired
1 egg yolk, well beaten, stirred in 1/4 cup plus 2 tablespoons
  lukewarm water
6-7 medium apples, peeled and sliced
6-7 tablespoons honey
butter
whipped cream, if desired

Preheat oven to 350°F; grease a torte pan with softened butter. Cut up stick of butter into a mixing bowl; add flour and sugar, and blend with a fork until it has the consistency of coarse crumbs. Add yolk and water, stirring mixture until it is moist; form into ball. Press dough into torte pan, spreading into place with fingers and fork. Cover dough with sliced apples, overlapping the slices in thick layers. Trickle honey over apples (be sure to cover apples completely with a thin coating of honey.) Dot apples with butter; bake for 50 minutes or until crust is golden brown. Serve hot or cold, with whipped cream on the side.

Elizabeth Lasher Clough
nonagenarian

"I can't convey why, but there's no place like Woodstock."

Elizabeth is a Woodstock native whose grandfather, father and brother were funeral directors in town as far back as the 19th century. Her husband was a writer and editor of a weekly Woodstock newspaper, **The Art Bulletin.**

"I had a great childhood," says Elizabeth, who was brought up on a farm where parents, grandparents, and siblings shared the work and fun. "I attended the stone schoolhouse that stood where the Grand Union is today. I went to school at the then-early age of 5, and I have a suspicion that my parents were happy I wanted to go."

The Lasher family was friendly with many of the Woodstock artists during the 1920s and 1930s, and works of Woodstock scenes grace the walls of Elizabeth's home. Her thoughts on the "Aquarian Age" participants are succinct. "The hippie era of Sixties didn't affect me," she says, contrasting that period with the time when the artists were flourishing in Woodstock. "But I do know that the artists boarded in houses throughout Woodstock; they didn't live under a spruce tree or sleep under a bridge."

When asked to reveal her recipe for a long life (she was 95 at the time of the interview), Elizabeth responded confidently, "My family always thought of me as a rabbit. I liked to go out and collect wild greens in the fields. If you sauté dock, it tastes better than spinach. I also enjoy picking and eating dandelion greens." And although she has lived away from Woodstock and traveled widely, she "always came back home. I can't convey why, but there's no place like Woodstock!"

CLOUGH CUSTARD

Elizabeth told us that she never particularly enjoyed cooking. "I don't know of a recipe I can give you" was her

39

first response to our request. But after consideration, she turned up what she calls "the best custard," one that "turns out perfectly every time." We can't think of a better recommendation.

2 cups milk
1/4 cup sugar
1/8 teaspoon salt
3 egg yolks, well beaten **OR**
2 whole eggs
1/2 teaspoon vanilla
1/8 teaspoon nutmeg

       Preheat oven to 325°F. Beat together all the ingredients. Pour into individual oven proof baking cups and bake for 1 hour or until a knife inserted into custard comes out clean.

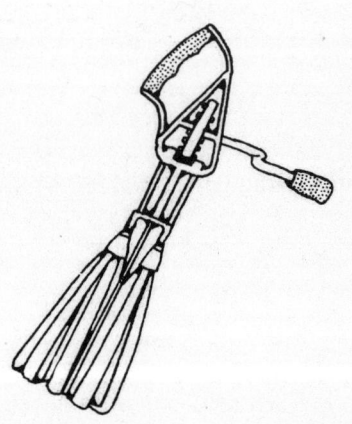

Peter Schickele
composer

"I think much more about malted milks than bottles of wine."

"How did I get to Woodstock? It was a fairly typical process, which according to one of my friends, works like this: you know someone, you rent, you buy, you think about moving up full-time...and then you move to California," says Peter, laughing. "Only I didn't move to California."

A warm, jovial man, Peter is a composer whose best known "composition" is none other that that long-lost chip off the old Bach, P.D.Q., although Peter has also composed music for dozens of shows, among them **Funny Man, Oh! Calcutta, The Crazy Quilt,** and has been the musical arranger for Joan Baez. Today, Peter comes to his Woodstock home each summer from Brooklyn, and then he rarely leaves the area except to go to local restaurants for a change of scene. "Back when the Bear was the Bear (Restaurant), I would go to the post office and then sit outside there by the stream and go through the mail," he says. After working for most of the day, Peter enjoys a change of pace. "I like scenes a lot, I love people-watching and I'm perfectly happy to go to Duey's for a cheeseburger or grilled cheese sandwich on Canadian Oat, which is my standard when I'm breaking up the day."

Although he was born in Ames, Iowa, Peter considers Fargo, North Dakota, his hometown; that's where he went to high school and where many of his friends still live. Peter's father was an agricultural economist who worked for the government, and the family spent time in the grainbelt and Washington, D.C. "I'm a Midwestern boy with Midwestern tastes," Peter says as he candidly considers his favorite foods. "I don't like seafood, and I don't particularly care for fish. I like corn, and I think much more about malted milks than I do about bottles of wine," he laughs. In fact, according to Peter, the Jackson Drugstore in Jackson, Wyoming, is one of the few places you can still get a great malted milk with homemade ice cream. "Two things I would probably die for are orange juice and ice cream," Peter reveals, and he goes

41

on to say that screwdrivers are his "grown up" drink of choice. As for the ice cream, it's Häagen Dazs coffee, although he never buys a cone to eat on the street. "You have to eat that ice cream at room temperature to get the best flavor and who wants to wait?" he wonders. In his opinion, a pint is the way to go.

Peter also loves pesto, Chinese food and avocados. He subscribes to the philosophy that everyone should have at least one item daily from each of the four basic food groups: sugar, salt, grease and chocolate. Predictably, Peter admits "desserts are my raison d'être." He describes his usual behavior when he goes into a bakery for dessert: "I never think about how hungry I am, but rather how I should get every kind of pastry since I have the irrational fear that they may stop making these items any day." Peter then expounds upon his feelings regarding bonafide desserts: "If I go somewhere for dinner and the dessert is cheese and fruit, I say to myself, 'What am I doing with these grown ups?'"

Obviously, cooking is not a focal point of Peter's life. "I have no knack in the kitchen; I do the washing up," he says, explaining that his wife, dancer Susan Sindall, does almost all the cooking. "The limit of complexity in my repertoire is adding curry to a basic hamburger casserole or making scrambled eggs." We couldn't resist asking Peter to describe what he would prepare if his pal P.D.Q. Bach was coming over to toss down a few screwdrivers. "For an appetizer, I would serve Campbell's Cream of Potato soup, and for the main course it would be Campbell's Cream of Asparagus."

Since Peter's on the road a great deal from October through March, and because he enjoys getting out of the house when he is working at home, Peter likes restaurants. "My favorite places aren't necessarily the ones with the best food, they're the ones with the best ambiance. What I like best about meals and restaurants is sitting around sharing food with friends." Even if it's just fried water.

FRIED WATER

(2-PART ROUND)

PETER SCHICKELE

MODERATE ($ = c. 144)

FILL A SKIL-LET WITH WAT-ER; TURN THE BURN-ER TO

'TIL THE WAT-ER IS COV- ERED WITH

FRY

HIGH:

BUB-BLES; ONCE MORE,

43

Maria Nardi

Bazar Fine Foods

"To a plain rice salad, I may add pignoli nuts, raisins, shrimp."

A former summer visitor to the area, Maria is the chef/owner of Bazar on Tinker Street, where lines form for a taste of her garlicky minestrone soup or her light-as-air feta spinach pie. But it was a long journey from Maria's childhood home near Parma, in northern Italy, to the large, sunny brick and tile kitchen of her Ulster County home.

Maria's life is filled with all the elements of the American success story. "I recommended a friend for a job at Bazar," she explains, "and when she backed out at the last minute, I felt guilty and took the job myself." At the time the shop was run by a nearby Zen monastery, but in 1983, Maria purchased Bazar. Now it has turned into a thriving family enterprise, a must-stop in town for those who love imaginative homemade dishes and baked goods.

Maria, a friendly, maternal woman, loves to see people enjoy food. No sooner were we seated at her kitchen table, than there appeared an antipasto platter, and a spinach pie. Ask Maria about food, and be prepared to sit back and listen for hours. She develops her house specialties by "adding and tasting as I go along. My minestrone soup won't taste exactly the same from day to day." And she doesn't use cookbooks, preferring to taste test instead. "To a plain rice salad, I may add pignoli nuts, then shrimp, and maybe raisins, peppers and onions until it all works! " she tells us.

At that point, Maria's daughter, Lisa, who also works at Bazar, chimed in saying, "My friends love coming here for dinner." As we finished our rum raisin cheesecake, which Maria just happened to have on hand, we could well understand why.

44

100% VEGETARIAN LASAGNA

This is one of the most popular dishes at Bazar, says Maria, who notes that she rarely gets requests from local customers for meat lasagna. Onions and carrots are used to sweeten the sauce, and the best results will come from using fresh lasagna noodles.

Filling

1 cup spinach, chopped (if using frozen spinach, sauté it quickly
   in a little butter and drain)
3 pounds ricotta cheese
2 cups grated mozzarella cheese
1 cup of any grated soft mild cheese (cheddar, monterey
   jack, muenster) **OR**
   1 cup grated parmesan
salt & pepper to taste
dash of nutmeg (Maria favors this spice in many of her recipes)

In a large bowl, thoroughly mix all ingredients together; set aside.

Sauce

1/2 cup olive oil
2 onions, peeled and finely chopped
3 garlic cloves, crushed
1 carrot, grated
5 or 6 porcini mushrooms, cleaned and sliced
3 sun-dried tomatoes
1 teaspoon fresh parsley, chopped
2 cups imported plum tomatoes
salt & pepper to taste

In a large saucepan, heat olive oil and brown the onions, garlic and mushrooms. Add remaining ingredients and cook for one hour over low heat, stirring constantly. Cool slightly and blend for 30 seconds in blender or food processor.

45

To Assemble

1 box lasagna noodles
grated parmesan cheese

Preheat oven to 350°F. Prepare the noodles according to package directions; drain. In a large, flat pan, arrange a layer of noodles, then add a layer of filling and a layer of sauce; sprinkle with parmesan cheese. Repeat all layers until pan is filled; top with parmesan cheese and bake for one hour.

Irwin Touster
painter

"I became a jiffy chef. "

"In the kitchen, my mother was neither interested in plenitude nor loving care, she was interested in speed," recalls Irwin, who is the chairman of the Fine Arts Department at the Parsons School of Design and the proprietor of the Millstream Motel. If there were a category into which his mother's cookery would fit, it would be "Jiffy Jewish," states Irwin. "She invented Jiffy Crepes Suzette and the Jiffy Blintzer." Jiffy cookery is based on neither the spoon, the cup, the ounce nor the pinch. It is based on just two measurements: "abitta" and "alotta."

Irwin's first real test in the kitchen came not as a chef, but rather as an artist. When first married, Irwin and his wife were preparing Swedish meatballs for dinner guests. Although the recipe tasted fine, the color was a particularly unappetizing gray. Irwin assured his wife that he could fix the problem with their set of vegetable colors. "With the arrogance that comes with years of painting and being male," he says, "I let fly half the contents of the tiny bottle of orange color into the pot." This left a mass of Swedish meatballs bobbing and bubbling in a thick, bright orange gravy. "I figured that what was needed were a few drops of blue," Irwin explains. This delicate balancing of color went on until the moment the guests arrived. "We ended up taking everyone out for dinner, and ate bright purple Swedish meatballs the rest of the week."

After this fiasco, Irwin gave up culinary painting. But his divorce forced him to face the kitchen alone. "It was then that I came to appreciate my mother's culinary philosophy. I became a jiffy chef."

THE LO-CAL JIFFY KNISH

"My mother served my Jiffy Knish with her famous Jiffy Brisket to a distinguished table of guests. When the wife of the Cultural Consul from Israel asked for the recipe, my mother declined, claiming she was sworn to secrecy," says Irwin. Now the secret is out, so enjoy.

Note: The traditional knish is wrapped in dough and deep fried; the jiffy knish contains far fewer calories.

"Take alotta mashed potatoes (a state-of-the-art jiffy chef will use French's Instant) and alotta soft fried onions and mix together. Fold in alotta freshly ground black pepper and abitta salt and garlic powder. Grease a cookie sheet and spoon out the mixture according to desired size. (I prefer cookie size and shape; make hearts for Valentine's Day.) Bake at 425°F until knishes are a deep golden brown. Serve hot." For a tasty variation, Irwin suggests inserting a cube of cheddar cheese into the center of the knish.

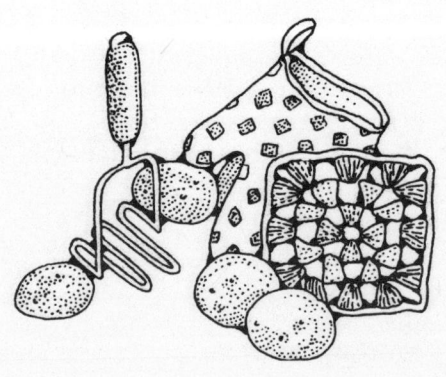

Bert Schultz

chef, KTD Tibetan Monastery

"Everyone here from Tibet loves Jello."

Bert Schultz is the chef at KTD, the only Western seat of one of the four lineages of Tibetan Bhuddhism. Located at the head of Mead's Mountain Road in Woodstock, the monastery is a peaceful place where the sounds of gongs and rhythmic chanting occasionally break the quiet.

Most of the time there are about 40 people (staff and guests) at the monastery for study and worship. The majority are Westerners, with only five or six Tibetans in permanent residence. Preparing three meals a day for such a diverse group is not easy. "I can't run out of food," jokes Bert, "or give someone a dollar and send them out for a hamburger!" He adds that there is usually a light breakfast and dinner with the main meal served at noon. The latter may include a dish of stir-fried beef with green peppers and pea pods, spinach, rice and a beverage.

"We're three-to-one, meat eaters to vegetarians," explains Bert. "All the Tibetans eat meat." Tastes differ between most Western and Eastern residents of KTD. "The Tibetans are accustomed to diets filled with heavy fats, oils, spices and one-bowl mixed dishes," Bert tells us. "If you don't know what you're doing in the kitchen, you can easily burn everything."

Along with being the chef, Bert also acts as prep person, storeroom manager and cook at the monastery. He is known there as the machen (ma shen'), which means "cook" in Tibetan. "When everyone particularly enjoys what I prepare," laughs Bert, "they call me machen chempo which means 'great cook!'"

Bert has been the chef at KTD since the mid-70s, almost as long as it has been an operating monastery. He was drawn there initially by his desire to attend one of the important celebrations known as a Black Crown Ceremony. Somehow, after that event, it became necessary for Bert to move there. "My original plan was to come for a few months, but I've been here ever since," he says. Bert was no greenhorn in the kitchen, however, since his culinary experience included a stint as chef at a London restaurant called The Flying Dragon. Despite its Oriental name, it was a "proper English tea shop," serving tea, scones, salads and sandwiches.

Although the monastery, atop a mountain, seems somewhat isolated from the Woodstock community and the rest of the world, some outside influences are unavoidable. "Jello," laughs Bert. "That is <u>really</u> big. Everyone here from Tibet loves it." Were there any other favorites? "Classic Coke!"

MEAD'S MOUNTAIN MOMO

Bert describes this dish as a hearty dumpling-type of meal that is traditionally accompanied by hot sauce (see following recipe.) Momo is served at KTD on special occasions like the Tibetan New Year.

Note: This recipe takes several hours to prepare and serves approximately 8 people.

3 cups unbleached flour
3 cups whole wheat flour
large pinch salt

Mix above with enough water to form a stiff dough. Form into ball, place in a large bowl, cover with a damp cloth and let rest 1 hour. Prepare filling (see below.) Remove dough and knead for approximately 5 minutes. Roll sections of dough into lengths about the thickness of a broomstick. Cut the "sticks" into 1 1/2" sections, and then roll out each section into a 4" circle. The circle should be slightly thicker in the center and taper towards the edges. Place 1 ball of filling in center of circle, and pinch the edges together to form a semi-circle; then pinch along the center of one side of the semi-circle to form a tricorne-shaped dumpling. (This sounds a lot more complicated than it really is.) To cook, use a steamer (metal or bamboo). Grease steamer bottom with oil to prevent dumplings from sticking. Place dumplings in steamer, at least 1/2" apart, and cook for 10 minutes at full steam. Remove to serving plate, and serve with hot sauce. (If you are using a steamer with more than 2 layers, rotate the layers during cooking to insure even steaming.)

Filling

2 pounds lean ground beef (have it ground twice if possible)
6 eggs
1/2 cup finely chopped onion
1 teaspoon salt
1/3 cup hot water
1/4 cup chopped scallion
1/8 cup chopped coriander leaves
2" piece of ginger, mashed (to mash ginger, Bert recommends
  putting it under a layer of plastic wrap and hitting it with
  a hammer.)

Mix all ingredients. Use 1 teaspoon for each momo, and form into balls.

YESHE NAMDA'S HOT SAUCE

Yeshe Namda, the chantmaster and ex-chef at KTD, passed this recipe along when Bert took over the kitchen. Bert substitutes fresh or canned tomatoes for the Ragu sauce that Yeshe liked to use.

1 small onion
1 tablespoon cayenne pepper
1 teaspoon salt
1 teaspoon ginger
half an apple **OR**
half a yam
2 large tomatoes **OR**
1 cup canned crushed tomatoes **OR**
1 16-ounce jar of prepared spaghetti sauce
1/4 cup water (if using fresh tomatoes)
fresh coriander leaves, if desired

Using a food processor or blender, blend ingredients into a smooth paste. Garnish with fresh, chopped coriander leaves if desired.

TRANSCENDENTAL TIBETAN TEA

This very strong and unusual tea, known as boeja in Tibet, is traditionally made in a churn. At KTD, it is prepared during holidays and milk is substituted for the heavy cream since Western tastes aren't accustomed to such a rich flavor. In Tibet, where the weather is quite dry, the leftover butter from the tea is used as a skin conditioner.

1/2 cup black Chinese tea
10 cups hot water
1/2 cup butter
1 cup heavy cream (you can substitute milk)
salt

Soak tea in water for 10 minutes, then boil for 15 minutes and strain. Add remaining ingredients, salt to taste, and blend mixture in a tabletop churn or a blender (you can blend 2 or 3 cups at a time.) Serve in cups.

A simpler version calls for putting a pat of butter and a dash of salt into a cup and adding hot, black tea.

Doug Grunther
radio talk show host

"I'm into peasant cooking."

Doug likes to explain the secret of fine cooking in one word: broth. "It's the basis of all good cooking, the distilled essence of taste," he believes.

By day, Doug is host of Woodstock radio station WDST's program, "Conversations." But after hours, Doug does all the cooking in his household and enjoys entertaining guests. "I grew up going to homes where the hosts didn't have fun at their own parties because they were worried about the soufflé not turning out just right," he says, adding that he prepares easy, one-pot meals for company that look good, taste great and don't require a lot of preparation. "I'm into peasant cooking, dishes that are either cooked quickly or simmered forever in one pot, so I can be part of the evening."

Doug describes himself as a "main course person" and dinner at his house is often a two or three hour affair. "I believe in the Symposium philosophy: eating, drinking and talking," he says. "Dinner is a wonderful place for this. At my house, guests arrive and it's 'Hi, how are you, let's eat.' I serve more food than most people can eat, and then more," he laughs. "If you don't have food left over, you've failed!"

Asked about culinary disasters, Doug recalled the "Woodstove Breakfast Mess." He bought a stove, complete with griddle, and invited friends over for a Sunday pancake brunch. "I poured the batter onto the griddle and it ran off all over the floor," he says. While wiping up the mess, his friends suggested that perhaps the stove wasn't hot enough, so Doug opened the vents and threw on the wood. This time around, with a roaring fire, the pancakes stuck. Solidly. "I was standing there, spatula in hand trying to pry them off the griddle," Doug laughs. He and his guests decided to eat out and Doug swears that when he later sold that stove, "the pancake batter was still on it!"

53

CONVERSATIONS WITH RED PEPPER PASTA

"My five favorite things in the world are red pepper, capers, garlic, olive oil and parsley," Doug says. Once, when in Chicago on a business trip, Doug ordered pasta with a sauce made from these ingredients and was disappointed in the flavor. "Everything looked beautiful, but it was just sort of lying there on the pasta." So at home, Doug used the same ingredients and was inspired to make this exciting variation on the original theme. **Note:** Doug always triples the amount of garlic in any dish he prepares, so adjust amounts accordingly.

garlic cloves
olive oil
sweet red peppers, roasted (you can do this by holding the peppers under a broiler until the skins are blackened, then peeling them)
fresh parsley, chopped
capers
prepared pasta of your choice

Sauté garlic in a little olive oil and set aside. In a blender, puree peppers and olive oil. Use enough oil to make a medium thick sauce. You can add more peppers or oil if needed and puree again. Mix in garlic, capers and parsley and blend until smooth. Serve over pasta.

CLOVE-LY BAKED BEANS

Beans are one of Doug's favorite foods, and he feels they are "underused in our society." The following recipe is what he would bring to a potluck supper. **Note:** This dish should not be attempted by those of you who go by the (cook)book. Wing it, and add all ingredients to your taste.

1 pound dried beans
vegetable stock or water
molasses
mustard (Doug recommends lots of this)
chili peppers, chopped
onions, sautéed
1 small can tomato sauce
1 small onion studded with cloves

       Soak beans overnight in water. Drain the beans, put them in a large pot, and add vegetable stock or water to cover. Bring to a boil and simmer for an hour; drain. Preheat oven to 350°F. In a large bowl, mix together beans, molasses, mustard, chili peppers, sautéed onions and tomato sauce. Pour into a casserole and put clove-studded onion in center. Bake for 1 hour.

Tepee (a.k.a. Barefoot) Bob
rugged individual

"I got tired of paying rent."

A fiercely independent man, Bob prides himself on leading a simple life. "I'm like Jesus," he says. "I gave away all my possessions, including my car. All I need are my bike, my shortwave radio and my tape recorder." With his red bandana and braided beard, Bob is a familiar sight around Woodstock.

He came to Woodstock from Spanish Harlem in 1968 through a friend's recommendation. At the time, he was in his early 20s, a Vietnam vet. He found a room in town for $20 per week and liked it so much that he went back to New York City, collected the rest of his things and hasn't been back since.

Bob's nickname comes from his unusual home: a tepee, which he built on Mt. Tremper after, he says, "I got tired of paying rent." He bought a book which guided him through the construction and has been living year-round in the tepee for almost twenty years. "I like to hear all the little voices and noises around me-- bears, deer, raccoons," he tells us. "I hear nothing but birds singing when I wake up in the morning. They don't come with commercial interruptions. The birds fill your dreams."

While winters are pretty rough, Bob has learned to appreciate what the season offers. "When a blizzard is coming and there are fifty-mile winds, it sounds like a subway overhead. But I can burrow into my furs, go to sleep and dream of Hawaii."

Despite the remote location of his tepee, Bob manages to be comfortable, even in the winter. Cooking is done in the middle of the tepee's floor on a wood fire. "I put three logs together and use a grill so that there's no smoke," he says. "I use a pressure cooker, although when it drops below zero, the steam will freeze to the side of the tepee's canvas."

Bob loves spicy food, and mentions cayenne pepper, curry and garlic as some of his favorite seasonings. He usually prepares simple, one-pot meals that require little liquid since he has to haul water in from a well almost a mile away, noting that "it's easier in winter when I use snow. I won't buy bottled water... or clouds or air, either."

Bob usually makes an annual trip to Kingston, saying that "I go there once a year for a Big Mac, to have something different." And he rarely makes the long bus trip to Baltimore to visit his family. Why? "My mother gets on my case about my not wearing shoes in winter."

Campers Take Note: The following recipes work as well on the trail as they do in a tepee!

TEPEE FRICASSEE

2 chicken breasts (approximately 1 pound total)
  and 2 legs or wings or thighs **OR**
1 small whole chicken
2 tablespoons paprika
1/2 teaspoon curry powder
1/2 teaspoon salt
water
1 cup sour cream
steamed rice, if desired

Mix together paprika, curry powder and salt and rub into chicken; let stand 5 minutes. In a covered frying pan, place chicken, any remaining spices and a small amount of water. Simmer for one hour or until meat is tender; you may have to add water (or snow) in 1/2 cup amounts. Remove the meat from the pan and stir in sour cream. Do not allow cream to boil or it will curdle. Serve over rice, if desired.

BAREFOOT BEEF STEW

1 pound beef, trimmed and cut into 2" cubes
2 carrots, peeled and sliced into "pennies"
2 potatoes, peeled and sliced
1 small onion, chopped
water
salt and pepper
1 can biscuit dough
water

In large covered saucepan, mix together beef, carrots, potatoes, onion, a small amount of water and salt and pepper to taste. Bring to a boil, reduce to a simmer and cover; cook for 1 1/4 hours or until beef is tender. Fifteen minutes before serving, roll the biscuit dough into 2" balls and drop into stew for dumplings.

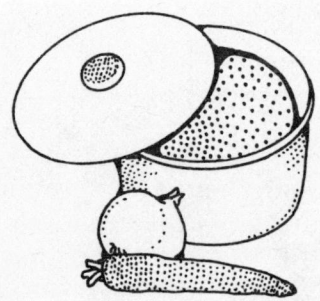

Suzanne Warner Pierot

producer

"I ended up working for Howard Hughes."

A cat may have nine lives, but Suzanne comes quite close. We couldn't possibly include them all, but here are some of the highlights...from the beginning. Her father died when she was three and her mother went to work as women's page editor at the **San Francisco Chronicle.** "I remember the day there was an earthquake, but my mother kept on typing because she had to meet her daily deadline," says Suzanne. Her mother was also one of the first women radio talk show hosts.

After graduating from high school, Suzanne wrote for movie fan magazines, but she was ever on the lookout for something more interesting. "One day I was at the beauty parlor and read an article in the **New Yorker** on Russell Birdwell, a top Hollywood press agent. I left the shop, drove to his office in Beverly Hills and announced to a very amused secretary that I wanted to work for Mr. Birdwell." Against all odds, Suzanne was hired.

One of Birdwell's clients was Howard Hughes and Suzanne became the publicity agent for his new film, "The Outlaw." Although the press party for the show was a distinct success, the movie was closed by the police. "I was almost arrested for purveying dirty films," laughs Suzanne, explaining how baring a little cleavage was considered risqué at the time. A court battle ensued, the film was vindicated and as Suzanne explains it, "Mr. Hughes liked the job I did and I ended up working for him; but in true Hughes fashion, we never actually met."

The following years were just as busy. Suzanne married, had a child and in between found time to become one of the founders of station ATV, the first commercial television station in England, a venture Sir Lew Grade was introduced to by Suzanne. Recalling those days Suzanne says, "I was a dealmaker, but I never handled deals or clients I didn't believe in."

After returning to America, Suzanne wrote several books on food and gardening and became one of the charter members of Les Dames Escoffier. It didn't surprise us that one book, **Suzanne's Cooking Secrets,** is a cookbook with no recipes, but is chockablock with time-saving culinary hints like "How to Avoid Garlic Hands," "The Paper Towel Trick for Fluffy Rice" and "How to Match Cake Layers."

One of Suzanne's more recent projects was producing Franko Richmond's **Tinker Street Suite** album, a collection of New Age jazz with a Woodstock theme, and she is currently researching a new book. As we left, Suzanne said with a wry grin that "I like to have several projects." An understatement, to be sure.

The following two appetizers may sound elaborate, but they are remarkably easy and will impress your guests.

CAVIAR RING A LA PIEROT

1 package unflavored gelatin
2 tablespoons dry sherry
2 tablespoons fresh lemon juice
6 hard-cooked eggs
1 cup mayonnaise
1 teaspoon anchovy paste
2 teaspoons Worcestershire sauce
one 2 1/2 ounce jar lumpfish caviar
parsley sprigs
sesame rice crackers or black bread

Generously grease a two-cup mold. In a small heat-proof container, soften gelatin in sherry and lemon juice for five minutes. Place over a very low flame and heat until dissolved, stirring several times. Chop eggs in blender or food processor and transfer to mixing bowl. Stir in gelatin, mayonnaise, anchovy paste and Worcestershire sauce; mix thoroughly. Gently fold in caviar, taking care not to break it. Turn into mold, cover and refrigerate until firm. Unmold and garnish with parsley sprigs; place crackers or bread around mold.

SIMPLE, SUMPTUOUS CHEESE CHUTNEY SPREAD

2 8-ounce packages cream cheese
1/2 cup mango chutney
1/2 cup chopped toasted almonds
2 tablespoons curry powder
1/2 tablespoon dry mustard

Blend all ingredients well and serve with crackers.

Heywood Hale Broun
commentator/journalist

"Apricots belong in an apricot whip-- not on your duck!"

After World War II, Woodie, as Broun is known to friends and family, started coming up to Woodstock from New York City, where he was working for a newspaper. "I bought a one room shack in 1947," he says, "and it has grown into a house." Two years later, in the summer of 1949, Woodie had his first on-stage job-- at the Woodstock Playhouse. "I played the part of the undertaker in a production of **I Remember Mama**, and ended up marrying the leading lady," (actress Jane Lloyd-Jones). They still live in the same house, which is now surrounded by rose and vegetable gardens and offers a stunning view of Overlook Mountain.

When the conversation turned to the kitchen table, Woodie mentioned that his love of gastronomy is inherited. His grandfather, a wine merchant, was a gourmet who lived on "alcohol, cholesterol and cigarettes" and died at the age of 88. He sold wines and liquors to restaurants, a job which also included sampling their cuisine.

Both Woodie and Jane enjoy cooking, and, according to Woodie, they keep "a little card file with all the dishes we've made up over the years," he says. "All of us in our family are good cooks." The Brouns have a vegetable garden, and one year they harvested more than 1,000 pounds of vegetables out of it. "We kept a diary and weighed the produce each day when we brought it in. According to Woodie, "you grow more tomatoes and less lettuce that way."

Broun is a world traveler and appreciates fine food, about which he has very definite likes and dislikes. "Apricots," he declares, "belong in an apricot whip, they don't belong on your duck. "He also feels that no other nation has ever equaled the French in cuisine. "They are <u>interested</u> in cooking; you can go to the equivalent of a diner there and have a great meal. In America, we think we have other things to do that are more important. Calvin Trillin was right when he said of many American restaurants that the food is 'La Maison de la Casa House international cuisine.'"

In general, Woodie avoids using cookbooks, saying "There are times when you have to use a cookbook; I use them for vegetable dishes, but on the whole I will use a cookbook when I'm bored with my own recipes. His favorite cookbook is the **Encyclopedia of Gastronomy**, where, he notes, "they tell you how to cook a lion and how to cook a rat, not that I'm going to cook either one, but that shows the breadth of the book." To Woodie, preparing food involves a willingness to take risks, and the cost of adventure, he admits, is an occasional failure, even in the kitchen.

The only time Broun felt like a true gourmet was at a restaurant in France where "they have terribly rich food, but you can't stop eating-- you just keep on." After the first course, a mousse, the chef came out to see what they thought of it. "It was so delicious, that Jane wanted me to say that her dream was to sit in a bathtub filled with this mousse and eat it all, then lick herself clean. My French is just fair, but I think I managed to convey the idea."

WOODIE'S ROUX THE DAY CASSEROLE

"Most of my specialties begin with some kind of roux or white sauce," says Woodie, "into which I dump coriander, mushrooms and other items. Like many who have had heart operations, I've become a veal and chicken kind of cook."

1/4 cup olive oil
1 1/2 pounds veal or chicken, boned, trimmed and cubed
1 tablespoon butter
1 tablespoon flour
1/2 cup chicken broth
1/2 cup white wine
1 teaspoon green peppercorns in vinegar (drain peppercorns and reserve 1/2 teaspoon vinegar)

Preheat oven to 350°F. In a heavy pan, brown veal or chicken in oil; drain and set aside. In a saucepan, melt butter, stir in flour until it is lightly browned. Gradually add broth and white wine to flour mixture, stirring constantly until well blended. Bring to a boil, reduce heat and simmer, stirring constantly, until sauce has thickened. Remove from heat and stir in green peppercorns and vinegar. Place veal or chicken in a casserole and pour sauce over it; bake for one hour.

THE RICHARD WALLER ONE-POT MEAL

This dish was named in honor of an English friend, who worked as a guide for Lindblad Tours and was introduced to the Brouns by S.J. Perelman. Waller was coming for dinner and Woodie and Jane didn't want to spend a lot of time cooking, so they devised this easy recipe. Woodie has also demonstrated it on television cooking shows.

olive oil
4 pork chops
1 cup white rice (not instant)
1 tomato, thickly sliced
1 onion, peeled and thickly sliced
1 large green pepper, seeded and sliced into rings
2 cups chicken broth
salt and pepper to taste

Preheat oven to 350°F. In a heavy casserole, brown the pork chops in olive oil; remove to a plate. Add rice to casserole and arrange pork chops on top. Put a slice of tomato, onion and pepper on each chop; pour chicken broth over chops. Cover and bake for 45 minutes.

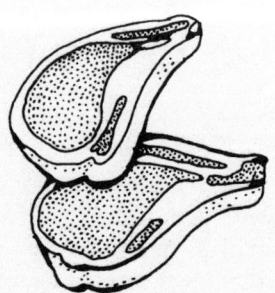

Robbie Dupree
musician

"I didn't even know where Woodstock was."

Anyone who has hummed the songs **Hot Rod Hearts** or **Steal Away** (which has been played more than a million times on the radio) will recognize Robbie's contributions to the world of light rock. He moved upstate from New York City in the Seventies. "First, I moved impulsively to New Paltz," Robbie says, explaining that he heard about the college there and figured the town would be a good place to live. "At the time, I didn't even know where Woodstock was," but after a couple of years, "the trail led naturally to Woodstock," says Robbie, who realized that "many of the best musicians I've ever met were living there." He moved to the town and eventually married Jeanne Port, a native Woodstockian. Today, Robbie offers an ironic reflection on the town's history, maintaining that "nothing Woodstock is famous for ever happened here, like the 1969 Festival and the Woodstock Art and Craft Fair, which is held in New Paltz. Everything the town is known for now is in the past."

When asked about his favorite foods, Robbie proves he has unique tastes in the Age of Nouvelle. "I'm the original terrible eater," he replies. "I like well-done meat, canned or frozen foods, nothing homemade and White Castle hamburgers, although they're hard to get out of the city. No one invites me for dinner more than once."

While Woodstock is known for its abundance of health food devotees, with two natural foods stores and only 7,000 people, Robbie refuses to compromise his values. "My Grand Union shopping cart could be considered pornographic in a place like Woodstock. I fill my wagon with Ben & Jerry's ice cream, Wonder Bread, all kinds of candy. I even buy the **Star** and the **Enquirer**," he admits proudly. Instead of a wine cellar, the Duprees converted their basement into a junk-food gastronome's version of Heaven. Some of the brand-name vintage delicacies stocked there include cans of Bosco, rows of Bonomo Turkish Taffy ("the dentist's best friend") and all flavors of Lik-A-Made. Robbie reveals that he is not alone in his dedication to vintage junk food: "We have friends who are just as crazy about this stuff as we are. Sometimes, when they come over, we just serve right from the basement."

TOAST AL BURNTÉ

This creation reminds Robbie of his childhood breakfasts, which he still enjoys at the age of 40.

2 slices Wonder Bread, with the crusts removed
2 pats Land O Lakes lightly salted butter
milk
Bosco

Toast bread to desired color, preferably black. Spread with butter and serve with milk and Bosco.

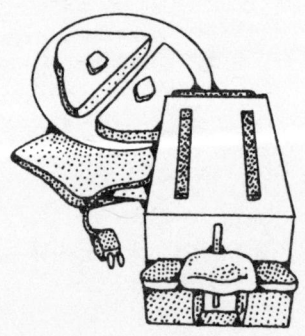

Bob Berman

astronomer

"The people are the jewels of any area."

How many astronomers could build their own observatory, complete with sliding roof that opens up to reveal the Woodstock heavens? And how many couid construct a rhombic triacontrahedron and then live in it? (For that matter, how many could even spell it?) Bob Berman has done all this-- and more. No ordinary scientist, he is also a licensed airplane pilot, a magician, tournament chess player and Scrabble aficionado. About his short-lived career as a builder, Bob says that "sheer bravado and naivete got me into it. I can only liken the job to what you would face if you had to build a working flying saucer." His unusual domed house, which looks as if it is floating above herb and flower gardens, is shaped somewhat like a 10-sided circle with no corners, a design chosen to echo the form of Bob's favorite place, the heavens.

Bob calls astronomy both his occupation and the love of his life, explaining the passion he discovered in childhood. After joining in what he calls "that extension of consciousness thing" in San Francisco during the mid-60s, Bob traveled around Asia, mostly by motorcycle "missing four years of Western civilization." He says, "There are still old songs my friends enjoy on the radio that I've never heard."

It was in Bombay that Bob experienced his most memorable dinner: "A family living on the streets invited us 'in' to share a meal, if you can imagine the sidewalks as a dining room. There were rats running by and trash in the gutters," recalls Bob, "but we were served with such pride, pleasure and dignity, that I still remember the food as being some of the best Indian cuisine I've ever had. The people are the jewels of any area."

After returning to the States, Bob continued his studies in astronomy, and on a visit to his sister in Woodstock, decided that the town suited him and there was no need to move on. Today, he lectures and teaches local classes in astronomy, as well as leading field trips around the world to the best spots for enjoying an eclipse or being dazzled by a supernova.

Bob senses that there is something "magical" about the Woodstock area, and this is why it's a perfect place to view the universe. "The skies here in the Catskills are like a living planetarium," he says. "The people Destiny has allowed to live here are also special: they have a buoyancy of spirit." To Bob, Woodstockians are "lovely, lively, wonderful, eccentric and bright." Just like the stars.

BOB'S STAR OF INDIA

"It was my misfortune to marry a wonderful cook," smiles Bob, as he explains why he doesn't do much cooking these days. Bob describes himself as "too impatient" to cook. "I eat all the ingredients before they even make it into the pot," he says. A hearty eater, Bob knows he's had enough when he 1) begins to see spots, 2) starts to hallucinate or 3) has difficulty breathing. One of the best things about Indian food, according to Bob, is that you can eat a lot and still feel great: "There is a mystical quality about it."

4 cups water
2 cups orange or green lentils
1 medium onion, chopped fine
salt, to taste
4 cloves garlic, chopped fine
1-2 tablespoons fresh ginger, chopped fine
2 tablespoons ghee (you may substitute an equal amount of safflower oil or peanut oil)
1 tablespoon curry powder
1 tablespoon cumin
1 teaspoon turmeric
1 teaspoon coriander seed
chili pepper, finely chopped, to taste
6 medium tomatoes, quartered
rice and plain yogurt, if desired

Cook lentils until tender; drain, add salt to taste and set aside. In a separate pan, sauté together the onion, garlic and ginger in ghee or oil; stir in curry powder, cumin, turmeric, coriander and chili pepper. Add tomatoes and cook on low heat for 10 minutes. Stir tomato mixture into the lentils; pour Spicy Butter (see recipe below) over mixture. Bob suggests yogurt and basmati rice as accompaniments to this dish, which serves 6-8 people. "If you really want to be authentic, eat it with your fingers," he laughs, "or go down to the pond and serve with water containing amoebas."

SPICY BUTTER

3 tablespoons butter
1 tablespoon curry powder
5 cloves garlic, chopped fine
1/4 cup chopped coriander leaves
2 tablespoons lemon juice

In a small saucepan, melt butter. Add remaining ingredients and stir over low heat until warm.

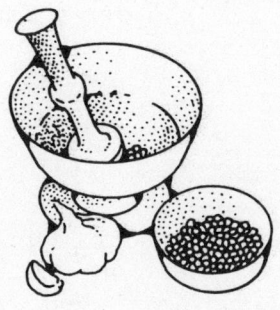

Paul & Heidi Draper
dancers

"We...imagined there were also orgies at the Maverick!"

A visit with Paul and Heidi Draper is like time-stepping into American dance history. Both studied with George Balanchine; in fact, the dance "Serenade" was choreographed especially for Heidi, who also danced in Broadway shows. Paul combined tap and balletic movement into his own unique dance style, and went on to star in top clubs like the Persian Room and Empire Room, onstage with monologist Ruth Draper (his aunt), and in the movie **The Time of Your Life** with James Cagney and William Bendix.

Introduced to Woodstock as a boy, Paul attended a camp on Witchtree Road, near an old mill. "We swam in the mill pond, lived in bungalows and on Saturday mornings, I'd go into town and peddle copies of **The Hue and Cry** for 10¢. Then it was time for a sundae at the drugstore and a ride back to camp. But," Paul reminisces, "the real dream of the campers, all boys of course, was to be old enough to attend a dance at the Maverick. We used to listen to local rumors and imagine that there were also orgies. I only hoped that if I were ever old enough, I could come back."

Eventually Paul did return, but as a worker on the Kingston Water Supply pipeline. "For one summer, I stayed with the Bonesteel family and every Sunday, we'd make fresh ice cream, and we'd all take turns cranking that wonderful stuff, which was flavored with fresh strawberries, peaches and vanilla. But I had to give thought to some other work, especially when my Aunt Ruth poked her head over a ditch one day and asked me what I was going to do with my life."

"What he did" was to eventually tour the world as a dancer and actor, which also gave him the chance to enjoy his avocation: fine food. Was there a secret dancer's diet that he followed to maintain his slim build? "I eat anything if I enjoy it," he laughs. "But I have a theory that dancers may be prone to certain psychological pulls. One night at a club, I ate lamb chops, spinach and mashed potatoes, and

I went out and did a sensational show. Of course, after that, I had to eat the same meal every night for the run!"

HOOFER'S HOLLANDAISE

Paul is justifiably proud of his fool-proof hollandaise sauce, and he told us this tale, along with the recipe.

"I was in Portland, Oregon, at an outstanding seafood restaurant. The dinner was delicious, but the hollandaise was of such low quality that I informed the maitre d' of the problem. He spoke to the chef, and they invited me into the kitchen to demonstrate the best way to make the sauce. Well, I agreed, and after finishing my dinner, throughout which I started to worry whether my sauce would flop, curdle or run thin, I went into the kitchen, where everything was waiting for me: butter, eggs, vinegar, lemons, the chef, and a bain-marie, which took me a minute to decide how to use. I soon had the ingredients whisked together, and the sauce started to get that lovely, velvet sheen. The flavor was wonderful, and that was one of the happiest moments of my life!"

2 egg yolks
1/4 pound sweet butter, cut into pats (keep chilled)
juice of 1/2 lemon
1 tablespoon and a dash of red wine vinegar
pinch of salt and pepper

Fill a sauté pan with water and bring to a boil, then reduce heat. Hold a small metal bowl so that just the bottom 1/2" is immersed in the water. Add egg yolks, then 1 pat of butter, whisking the mixture until the butter is blended. Alternate the remaining pats of butter with teaspoons of lemon juice and vinegar, making sure the butter is thoroughly blended after each addition and the sauce takes on a velvet sheen. Whisk in the pepper and salt to taste. Serve the sauce warm.

PAUL'S BETTER BEARNAISE

This sauce is also easy to make and Paul recommends serving it over steak for an outstanding main course.

1/4 cup vinegar
3/4 cup red wine
a handful (about 1/2 cup) fresh tarragon OR
2 tablespoons dried tarragon
3 shallots, chopped
2 egg yolks
1/4 pound sweet butter, cut into pats
salt and pepper to taste

Put vinegar, wine, tarragon and shallots into a small sauce pan; bring to a foaming boil. Strain the liquid, and set aside the shallots and tarragon. Proceed as for the hollandaise sauce (see preceding recipe), substituting the wine and vinegar liquid for the lemon and vinegar. Serve the sauce over steak, using the reserved shallots for garnish.

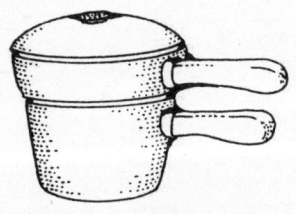

Sally Avery

artist

"Milton was usually totally unaware of what he was eating."

"I decided when I was five years old that I would be an artist," Sally explained one afternoon in her studio/home. What she couldn't foresee was her part in encouraging and promoting the career of husband Milton Avery, a role she assumed after meeting the artist at a summer arts colony in Massachusetts, and which continued until his death in 1963 (He is buried in the Woodstock Artists' Cemetery.)

The walls of Sally's Woodstock home are covered with her large canvases, landscapes and still-lifes painted in warm colors reflecting her own vision, but sometimes reminiscent of Milton's work.

The Averys originally settled in Woodstock during the early 1960s in order to have a place to paint that was close to New York City. They had visited the town frequently since the 1940s and were friends with other artists including Arnold Blanch and Doris Lee, who, according to Sally, were "the king and queen of Woodstock at the time."

Milton's disinterest in food, as well as anything else besides painting, was legendary. "Why talk when you can paint," was his philosophy, which also extended to eating. Sally recalls that during the leaner times in their careers, visitors to their home would chip in for food. "Milton was usually totally unaware of what he was eating," Sally says. "He could eat the same thing day in and day out." One time when Sally was chatting with some other mothers at her daughter, March's, school, a woman asked Sally what she prepared for dinner. "I make hamburgers," she said. When asked what else she made, her reply was "I just make more hamburgers." (The secret to Sally's hamburgers, by the way, is to add almost nothing to the meat and to handle it as little as possible.) But Sally isn't shy about her limited culinary repertoire. "We were just interested in painting; everything else was peripheral."

STILL LIFE WITH CUCUMBER

Although hamburger was an Avery staple, this recipe (a favorite of March, also a painter) dates back to the summer of 1949, when the Averys lived in Millbrook, NY. They often dined at a Hungarian restaurant there, and enjoyed this unusual variation on the mundane vegetable.

1 large cucumber, peeled and thinly sliced
1 tablespoon chopped fresh dill
2 tablespoons butter
1/2 cup plain yogurt or sour cream
paprika, if desired

In a shallow pan, sauté cucumber and dill in butter for three minutes or until cucumber is translucent. Remove to serving dish and arrange in rows by overlapping each cucumber slice. Spoon yogurt or sour cream over the cucumber; sprinkle with paprika, if desired.

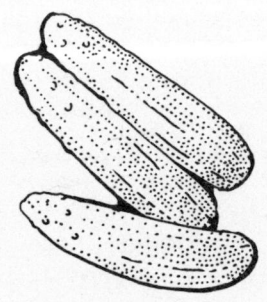

Robert Angeloch
founder, Woodstock School of Art

"I prefer the bare seasons to summer, when it's green, green, green."

The owner of the Paradox Gallery, Robert Angeloch, is a familiar figure around town in his jaunty country caps, but he dons other professional hats as well, including that of teaching at the Woodstock School of Art. "I would tell my students about the early Woodstock artists, but then I realized there was no place to go to see their work," he explained. This was one of the reasons he opened the Paradox Gallery; another, the chance to show his own work on a regular basis.

Woodstock has been home to Robert and his family since the early 1950s; he had come to study art in 1948 and decided to stay. His paintings include luminous still lifes and large canvases of Catskill landscapes. Some of his most striking landscapes are scenes of winter and early spring on the mountains, when leaf-stripped trees and grey-blue shadows rule. "I prefer the bare seasons to summer, when it's green, green, green," he says. "It can get pretty boring and I have to make up colors to get some relief."

Robert actually got into cooking only after he and his first wife split up. At the time, his children would visit on weekends, and a family ritual evolved. "We decorated a place in the house and called it Roberto's Ristorante, and each weekend we would change the menu," he explained. "It was silly, but we enjoyed it, one weekend it was Spanish cuisine, the next weekend, Italian."

When asked about his favorite foods, Robert prefaced his answer by telling us that because of his health, what he eats and what he likes are quite different...except for occasional splurges. "I love pasta of all kinds and heavy sauces," he confesses, "and I could eat sweets after every meal - breakfast, lunch and dinner."

Today, Robert is likely to turn out a tomato-y goulash, in his own special blend of food and art. On our way out, we couldn't help but notice a striking still life with pears which was hanging in the gallery. When we admired it, Robert told us that the fruit was wax. So much for truth in art.

MOTHER ANGELOCH'S GOULASH

The following recipe is a favorite from Robert's mother, a German cook of the old school.

2 pounds beef shoulder, trimmed and cubed (you can substitute chuck or sirloin, but Robert likes a shoulder cut best)
2 tablespoons butter
salt and pepper to taste
1 large onion, finely chopped
1 8-ounce can tomato sauce
water
1 tablespoon cornstarch dissolved in 1/4 cup water
flat noodles, if desired
boiled red cabbage, if desired

In a large heavy pot, brown the beef in butter; season with salt and pepper. Add onion and sauté. Pour in tomato sauce and enough water to cover beef mixture; bring to a boil and reduce heat. Add cornstarch/water mixture to pot and stir until mixture thickens. Simmer over low heat for 1 hour. Robert suggests serving this dish over flat buttered noodles, and adding a side dish of boiled red cabbage.

Bruce Gibson

all that the name implies

"I used to wear suits every day that looked like I was born with them on."

Every village has its characters, the people who refuse to fade into the background, and Bruce Gibson belongs to Woodstock. When we met Bruce on August 17, 1987, he had been up all night playing drums for the Harmonic Convergence. Our interview took place in his "office", a bench on the Village Green, where Bruce can be found every day, from "9 a.m. until 7:30 p.m. or until the last bus pulls out of town." You can't do justice to a description of Bruce. But you can experience an hour or so of his stories, since he's always glad to talk about himself and Woodstock to anyone who cares to stop by his bench.

Born in New Jersey in 1940, Bruce grew up in Ohio and came to Woodstock in 1967, after working as a publicity agent for United Artists. Other jobs included managing several Greenwich Village cafe kitchens, among them Cafe Wha, and playing guitar and drums in various groups.

Bruce's New York City lifestyle was a far cry from his laid back ways of today. One of his apartments was just downstairs from Faye Dunaway's, another was at the fashionable community of Seagate. "I had a friend with a mistress whose wife was getting suspicious," Bruce smiled, in recalling the past. "So he asked me to share an apartment with him there as long as I disappeared on Thursdays." Today, Bruce chooses to put comfort before style in clothing, but that wasn't always so. "I used to wear suits every day that looked like I was born with them on," he says, shaking his head and laughing. "I went to a show business tailor who would fit you three times to get the suit just right." Bruce reminded us to look at the album cover of "Tinker Street Suite," produced for the Woodstock Bicentennial, where he is suited up for the camera.

Bruce was a member of a band, All That The Name Implies, which toured with The Doors and Earth Opera in the Sixties, and his move to Woodstock resulted from a suggestion made by the band's manager. "We had just finished a gig early one morning," recalls Bruce, "and it was August and we couldn't go home to sleep, so we wandered around the Sheep Meadow in Central Park. I called our manager to see if he wanted to have a barbecue, and instead, he asked us to come with him to visit some friends in a small town called Woodstock. When we got there, I took one look at Overlook Mountain, and moved up seven days later."

Once in Woodstock, Bruce continued to play in his band and manage cafes including The Purple Elephant (now Elephant Emporium) on Rock City Road. Bruce still recalls a night in 1967 when Jimi Hendrix, the Paul Butterfield Blues Band and Santana all stopped by to jam. "I fell asleep somewhere in the early morning and one of my assistants woke me later to tell me that something was wrong with the building. I thought, Oh, hell, what could be wrong with a building, but when I followed him outside, sure enough, there had been so much dancing that the building shifted about three feet off its foundation!"

Bruce and the band members lived communal style in Woodstock and although "the girls did most of the cooking," Bruce occasionally "got creative." He describes his culinary modus operandi as getting "the spices, everything, down from the shelves and then just going for it. I could be in there for half the day and no one could get me out."

One of Bruce's favorite brunch dishes is Tuna Fish Pancakes. We couldn't get him to reveal the exact recipe, but this seems to work: mix together a can of solid white tuna (drained), a little sour cream, some pancake mix, a touch of baking powder for fluffiness and the juice of half a lemon. "Delicately season with white wine," advises Bruce, "and serve along with spaghetti with white clam sauce and a dry riesling."

BRUCE'S BENCHBURGERS

All That The Name Implies lived at Byrdcliffe for a while "because it was cheap." During his Byrdcliffe cycle, writes Bruce, "I did a bit of kitchen creating and this became a favorite among the communal crazies." The dish has a spicy Polynesian flavor, and recommends Bruce, "if you're a veggie, serve it to someone carnivorous."

3 pounds lean chopped sirloin (chopped fresh to order at Woodstock Meats)
6 tablespoons teriyaki sauce
1 1/2 teaspoons Chinese mustard
1/2 teaspoon paprika
16 fresh scallions, finely chopped
2 tablespoons vegetable oil
1 clove garlic, crushed
18 strips thick, smoked bacon
6 pineapple rings
12 slices of cheese (Bruce prefers extra sharp cheddar)
6 large sesame seed buns, sliced
1 pint cherry tomatoes
a few sprigs of fresh parsley

Preheat oven to 350°F. In a large bowl, mix together the meat, teriyaki sauce, Chinese mustard and paprika. In a wok, cook the scallions in vegetable oil. Add garlic and cook for a minute; remove and drain. Blend this into the meat mixture. Form six half-pound patties; brown on both sides in the wok. Place patties on a greased cookie sheet and bake in oven for twenty minutes. While they are baking, cook the bacon in the wok; drain. When patties are done, remove from oven and top each patty with three strips of bacon, a pineapple ring and two slices of cheese. Return to oven until cheese is melted. Serve on toasted buns; garnish with tomatoes and parsley. Bruce suggests serving this with stir-fried Chinese vegetables, Peppers and Skins (see recipe), yogurt, Chinese almond cookies and tea.

PEPPERS & SKINS

5 pounds baking potatoes
4 pounds bell peppers
vegetable oil
sweet and sour sauce, if desired

      Peel and save the potato skins ("do what you want with the potatoes.") Slice the peppers into thin strips. Using a wok, saute the potato skins in oil until they are crisp and brown, then add the peppers for a minute. Serve in a basket with sweet and sour sauce on the side.

Note: You can reduce this recipe by using only 1 potato and 1/2 a pepper per person.

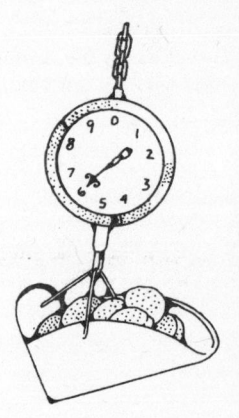

Gail Godwin & Robert Starer

novelist & composer

"We're old-fashioned: Gail cooks and I clean up."

Gail Godwin's incisive, graceful prose is familiar to readers of her novels, which include **A Southern Family, The Finishing School,** and **A Mother and Two Daughters,** but she is also a librettist, having written the libretti for two one-act operas, **The Last Lover** and **Apollonia.** Robert Starer is one of America's leading composers, who has written works for orchestras, chamber groups and the ballet, including **Samson Agonistes,** composed for the Martha Graham dance troupe. And like Gail Godwin, he has crossed into other creative fields, as the author of **Continuo,** a wise, often funny, autobiography of his musical life.

Gail and Robert moved to Woodstock from Stone Ridge to a home where, in the times between their creative hours, Robert admits they lead a somewhat regular life. "I'm afraid," he laughs, "that we're old-fashioned: Gail cooks and I clean up. She's a wonderful cook. The only thing I can do with food is to make cheeseburgers on Sunday. But since I have always written very early in the morning, and she sometimes works very late, I do bring her coffee in bed."

Robert is thoughtful when asked to recall his most memorable meal. It was during World War II, when he was performing as a concert pianist. "We gave a concert for Lord Moyne, who was later assassinated. The other musicians and I were so hungry, there wasn't much food available in those days, that at dinner we ate and ate. Some of us even put food in our pockets to take home. But since I was unused to that much food, for three days after, I was ill."

With Gail's Southern roots and Robert's Austrian, Israeli and American background, does dinner get interesting around their house? Gail says that her cooking is simple, with Southern touches, although Robert has introduced his favorite veal dishes to the menu. "I may have told her about the dishes, but she developed the recipes," he explains. "Unfortunately, every time I turn to cooking, the veal comes out black. It has something to do with the oil being much too hot...or not hot enough. Something like that. Anytime I'm in the kitchen, it's a disaster." Fortunately, it was Gail who provided the following recipes, in her own distinctive style.

A SOUTHERN FAMILY'S FRIED CHICKEN

Like anyone who knows anything about real Southern food, Gail is very specific about fried chicken. "I got this recipe from a black woman who treated cooking as an effort of love. It's the right way to fry chicken."

"Take a brown paper bag (it has to be a tough brown bag, use two bags if necessary) and put flour, salt and pepper in the bag. Drop the chicken in the bag and shake (this is the best way to dredge it.) Put some oil in a heavy frying pan and heat it; the best way to see if the oil is hot enough for cooking is to flick a drop or two of water in the oil. If it goes "phfft" and dances around on the oil, then it's ready. This is where people make a mistake. If the oil isn't hot enough, the chicken just sits there and gets greasy. Just be sure not to burn the oil. Add the chicken, and it should start sizzling right away. Now comes the difficult part. Most people just turn the chicken once while it's cooking, but you have to stand there and keep turning the chicken until it's done. Stay with it, just like a baby, and don't think about anything else until it's finished cooking. Sometimes, if I want to impress my friends, I may marinate the chicken in lemon juice for a few hours before cooking it. It gives the chicken a different flavor, and people say 'Oh, what is this?' with the first bite."

NOVEL POACHED SALMON

"I go to the Grand Union and get salmon filets (not steaks) for this dish. Take a big, black frying pan (that's Southern), add some water and put it to boiling. If I have fresh herbs from the garden, I add thyme and oregano, and lemon juice and some lemon peel also. When the water is boiling, add the salmon and boil for just 7 minutes-- any more is too much. Drain the salmon and serve it with salsa verde, boiled new potatoes or a couscous salad. I add dates, raisins, carrots, zucchini and onion to the couscous, and serve it all over kale, not collard, greens."

SENSATIONAL SALSA VERDE

"The basic recipe for this came from Rick Schneller (of Schneller's Meat Market, in Kingston), but I've added some things to it as well. You have to do it instinctively, by taste, and you can use a blender or food processor. Put parsley, dill, capers and some garlic in the blender, then crunch it up. Slowly add olive oil to the mixture and serve over poached salmon."

Abigail Robin

entrepreneur

"In Woodstock, you were either an artist or a native."

"At night after working as a camp counselor upstate, I would get into my '57 Chevy and drive either to the Village Vanguard in the city or the Cafe Espresso in Woodstock," says Abigail, explaining how she was first introduced to the town in the Sixties. "I was enthralled with the arts colony," she remembers, and thus it was that she and her then-husband, Steve, moved to Woodstock after college. But Abigail also recalls an unusual problem she faced in her new home. "I felt absolutely isolated. In Woodstock, you were either an artist or a native, and I was an English teacher."

She soon felt more at home with the arts world, and quit her job to work at weaving and ceramics, as well as an artists' representative. One of her first clients was Steve, who was working full time as a woodworker, and needed a way to sell his art. Abigail decided to hold an unusual "home party," to sell what they would later call Furniture as Art. "It was like a tupperware party," she says laughing, "only there were mirrors, tables and chairs instead of kitchen containers." The idea worked, and Abigail wrote more than $1500 worth of orders, "a lot of money at the time."

In 1981, Abigail became the area representative for a friend who ran tours of Manhattan art galleries and needed someone in the Woodstock area. After guiding her first town tour, Abigail was stunned when her clients showed their enthusiasm. "People stood up and applauded at the end," she says. "I thought, 'Oh my God-- I can be a stand-up comedienne, actress and tour guide all at once.'" Not long after, Abigail launched ART (Abigail Robin Tours), one of the best ways for people to go behind the scenes in Woodstock and visit artists' studios, galleries and the cultural hotspots.

MAGIC RUSSIAN CAVIAR

"When I moved to Woodstock," remembers Abigail, "the first person I met was Sylvia Elias. At her house, I usually found Sylvia in front of the stove whipping up a meal for a few artists who were coming to dinner. Her husband, Fred, served the drinks and spiced up the evening with intellectual inquiry and fierce, friendly argument. I would watch as Sylvia transformed simple eggplant into Russian caviar."

1 eggplant
1 large onion, quartered
1 large clove of garlic, chopped
1 tablespoon olive oil
juice of half a lemon
1 tomato, diced
salt to taste
crackers, if desired

Preheat oven to 350°F. Pierce the skin of the eggplant with a fork. Place in a pyrex dish filled with about 1 inch of water and bake the eggplant until softened. Peel the eggplant and chop into small pieces in a wooden bowl. Add the onion and garlic and chop some more. Stir in the olive oil and lemon juice until the mixture has the quality of "herringbone tweed." Add tomato, salt and serve chilled with crackers.

ABIGAIL'S ARTFUL ARTICHOKES

Abigail considers cutting the tips off artichokes "an exercise in meditation." This recipe provides the cook with both an entree and a soup...as well as time to meditate.

"Cut the tips off some artichokes. Put them into a large pot along with 4 cups of water, some olive oil, 3 cloves of garlic (squeeze them into water, first), and sliced onions. You can chop up some spinach, kale and broccoli, (all the green, healthy things) and throw them into the pot as well. Squeeze in some lemon juice. Bring the soup to a boil, then reduce the heat and let it simmer for 40 minutes or so. If you want, you can strain out the vegetables for a meal and use the liquid as a vegetable stock in other recipes."

Philip Elwyn
proprietor, Deanie's Restaurant

"There used to be four stools, a couple of booths and no liquor."

Deanie's Restaurant has been an elegant Woodstock watering hole for more than half a century, attracting the famous, the not-so-famous and the sometimes infamous. Philip Elwyn, present proprietor of the restaurant started by his father and grandmother, can reel off the names of well-known patrons of Deanie's over the years, including Dylan, Cher, Mama Cass, Jimi Hendrix, Lee Marvin, Celeste Holm, and Robin Williams. "There are a few soap opera stars...and a porn star that I don't know but others have told me about," he smiles.

The place opened in 1936 in a trolley car where Tinker Square is located. "There were four stools, a couple of booths and no liquor was served," says Philip, who explained that over the years the restaurant was renovated several times. Deanie's mother was an excellent cook and baker, so mother and son worked together in the business. In 1973 a fire forced the Elwyns to find a new location for the restaurant. They ended up purchasing the building they presently occupy and opened for business in 1974.

As far as specialities of the house, diners at Deanie's fancy drinks like Irish Coffee with freshly whipped cream. And talking about cream brings Philip to one of Deanie's extraordinary desserts, Banana Cream Pie, which is still made from a 1936 recipe of his grandmother's. "We sell a ton of it," Philip says. But you will have to go to Deanie's for this treat, since Philip is understandably reluctant to divulge the recipe. However, we settled for another spectacular treat, Piña Colada Pie, which was added to the menu in 1987. And judging from the taste, Philip may be just a little sorry he gave this one away so easily.

DISCO LINDA'S EASY PINA COLADA PIE

Linda Sheldon (a/k/a Disco Linda of The Lake) is the prep chef at Deanie's who does all the baking. She added the lemon pudding to the original recipe and advises that "yellow rums work best for baking." The recipe yields THREE 8" pies, so divide for smaller amounts.

one 3 1/2-ounce package instant vanilla pudding
one 3 1/2-ounce package instant lemon pudding
1 cup sugar
2 cups sour cream
one 20-ounce can crushed pineapple, drained
4 cups shredded coconut
2 teaspoons grated lime rind
6 tablespoons Mount Gay rum
three 8" baked pie crusts
freshly whipped cream, if desired
fresh orange wedges, if desired

In a large bowl, mix the puddings and the sugar. Add sour cream, pineapple, coconut, lime rind, and rum and mix well. Pour into baked pie crusts. Refrigerate for three hours. Serve topped with fresh whipped cream and orange wedges.

AN IRISH COFFEE FILLIP

1 1/4 ounces Bushmills Irish Whiskey
1 teaspoon sugar
freshly brewed coffee
freshly whipped cream

Stir the whiskey and the sugar into the coffee; top with whipped cream.

John Herald
bluegrass musician

"I've always been interested in hunting mushrooms."

John grew up in Greenwich Village, where his father was a poet, but his introduction to the Woodstock area came with summers spent at the Peter Pan Farm on Glasco Turnpike and at Camp Woodland in nearby Phoenicia. Today, John is a well-known bluegrass musician with his own band, and has recorded and performed with Bob Dylan, James Taylor, Bonnie Raitt, Joan Baez, Paul Butterfield and Jackson Browne, among others. Co-author of the Peter, Paul and Mary hit "Stewball," John can also claim the arrangement of Linda Ronstadt's first big single, "Different Drum." His music is a blend of old and new country, bluegrass, folk, Cajun and swing, and except for a short California phase, John has lived in Woodstock since the Sixties.

An unusual musician, John also has an unusual hobby. "I've always been interested in hunting mushrooms, and in 1968 I started to seriously study them," he explains. "The first year I used a book which turned out to be about mushrooms native to Michigan, so I wasn't able to identify too many varieties around Woodstock," he recalls, smiling. But with the proper books and several years of hiking, looking and studying, John developed a knowledge of scores of local fungi. "I've tried about 45 different types of local mushrooms out of the perhaps 100 edible ones, including the pinewood boletus, morels, chicken mushrooms and lacterius indigo. Of the thousands of species, most are not edible; either they are inedible because of taste or texture, or they are slightly to deadly poisonous."

Mushroom gathering isn't an exact science, according to John. "One can rarely make generalizations about mushrooms," he explains, saying that there are no clear-cut rules to follow to know for sure that one is safe to ingest and another is not. "You have to know exactly what it is you're looking at." Although some mushroom poisons can be eliminated in the cooking process, John recalls an early attempt at collection, when he and some mycologist

88

friends gathered and cooked a mushroom that was listed in one book as poisonous, and in another as edible. The mushrooms ended up making him, and a couple of dinner guests, ill, but fortunately, this was his only bad experience in twenty years of tasting.

In the Woodstock area, the best mushrooming season is from late July through September, when the fungi can be found on lawns, in woods and meadows, "just about any place." If they are not fresh looking or have bruises or wormholes, "don't mess with them," advises John. He usually takes two plastic bags with him when hunting: one for the mushrooms he recognizes and one for those he doesn't. To clean the mushrooms, wash them carefully under the faucet with cool water, then drain on paper towels. They should be eaten the same day they are picked, or cooked and then frozen. Some mushrooms can even be preserved by putting a screen over a wide lamp shade and spreading the mushrooms out on the screen; the heat from the light bulb dries them. And John recommends cooking one species of mushroom at a time to better enjoy the separate, distinctive flavors.

John showed us a jar of morels that he had collected and dried for snacks. "These are great if you break them into mushroom 'chips' and add salt," he laughs. "I can't figure out why no one has come up with that snack yet and given the potato chip industry a run for its money."

NOTE: Do not attempt to collect and eat local mushrooms unless you are absolutely sure of their identity. Although there are many mushrooms that are safe to eat, others can cause extreme discomfort and even death. The following recipe is for those people who are experienced in mushroom identification.

BLUE STEW

One of the easiest mushrooms to identify is lacterius indigo. "The cap is a dull blue-green to a silvery grey with moist, fading concentric circles and the stem and gills are colored the same," says John. "It's the only mushroom that exudes a blue 'juice' or latex when cut or nicked." (These mushrooms shouldn't be confused with those that turn color when <u>bruised</u>.) If you think you've found lacterius indigo but are unsure of the identification, feel free to give John a call and he will be glad to help you out.

To prepare the "stew," clean and slice the mushrooms. Sauté for several minutes in a couple of tablespoons of peanut oil and salt to taste (other oils may be used, but John feels peanut oil is best.) The cooking liquid will retain a natural blue-green color from the juice, so don't be alarmed.

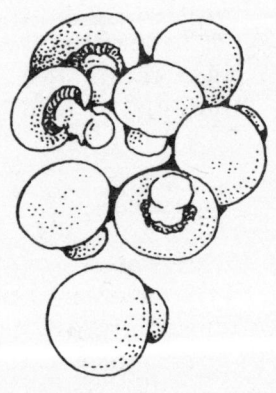

Betty Ballantine
publisher, Ballantine Books

"We had chickens, goats and a water buffalo for milk."

Betty met her husband, Ian, in 1939, while living in the Channel Islands. Although they wanted to marry, her father was adamant about Betty's not leaving England with her American beau until he had a job lined up in the States. Ian solved the problem by becoming the American representative for Penguin Books, and Betty traveled to New York. "There were three of us-- Ian, a stock boy and myself," remembers Betty. "We often worked sixteen hour days, and sometimes had to haul 50,000 books up the stairs to our office from the street... We even built the bloody shelves ourselves."

During World War II, when it was difficult to import quality books, the Ballantines began producing their own titles. The first book, **What's That Plane?**, was an identification manual of Japanese aircraft for the American market, although much of the information had to come from the British Navy, which was more fully prepared for war. Later, when the Ballantines had their own firm, they published as original paperbacks a wide list of general fiction and non-fiction, including several ecologically conscious cookbooks.

Born in India, where her father worked for Britain's Opium Department, Betty recalls rural life where cooking was done on a charcoal stove and electricity was non-existent. "Everything was homemade out of necessity," she explains. "My mother even made her own talcum powder from orrisroot. I was always very conscious about food and where it came from; we had chickens and goats, and a water buffalo for milk. Our food was literally 'on the hoof.' When you moved, you took the animals with you."

Betty's mother was responsible for a household of about fifty people, including the head cook and assistants. Refrigeration, a problem in India, was tackled with creativity and even a sense of style. "We had great big nets of aromatic fibrous roots suspended over the porch, and our crocks and bottles would be placed in the netting. A bucket of water was kept nearby, and every time you passed the net, you would throw water over the net and give it a push so it would sway in the breeze and cool the bottles."

But despite her exotic background, Betty is still a stalwart defender of British cooking. Before the war, she feels, there might have been grounds for criticism, but afterward, the Continental influence and influx of immigrants has given Great Britain "a place among the world's great cuisines."

BB's CURRIED MONKFISH

1 onion, peeled and sliced
1/2 cup vegetable oil
1 tablespoon washed red lentils
4 tablespoons converted white rice, uncooked
1 heaping teaspoon hot Madras curry powder
2 rounded teaspoons ground cumin
1 green pepper, chopped
1 tomato, chopped
1/2 cup chopped celery
fresh basil
garlic salt
a few raisins
1 can chicken broth, undiluted
additional water as needed
juice of 1/2 lemon
1 pound cut up monkfish

In a large pot, sauté onion in oil until soft. Add all dry ingredients, and follow with chopped vegetables and liquids except lemon juice; do not add fish. Cook over a low heat for 10 minutes. Add lemon juice and fish, cover and cook for 20 minutes, mixing occasionally. Serves 4.

TANGY TOMATO CHUTNEY

Chutney is a spicy relish made with fruits. Betty loves this one because it's easy to prepare and can be kept in the refrigerator or canned for longer storage.

2 heads (approximately 10 cloves) garlic
1 1/2 cups peeled fresh ginger
1/2 pint apple cider vinegar
12 hot green chili peppers
2 limes
1/2 pound raisins
1/2 pound dark brown sugar
2 teaspoons dry mustard
1 teaspoon mixed spice (use apple or pumpkin pie spice mix)
1/2 teaspoon ground cardamom
4 quarts cherry tomatoes

Coarsely chop garlic and ginger; add vinegar. Finely chop chilis and limes. Put all ingredients into a large pot and cook very slowly (about 3 hours) until sauce is reduced by a third. Cool and store in the refrigerator or pour into sterilized jars and seal according to manufacturer's directions.

Mary Frank
sculptor

"Only in America would you cultivate a fruit you don't eat!"

Mary's distinctive clay sculptures reflect a special vision of women as ancient, mysterious beings; indeed, the sculptures are often named after mythic characters. She is also well-known as a painter and children's book illustrator, and her works are represented in many private and public collections, including the Museum of Modern Art, the Metropolitan Museum of Art and the Whitney-- as well as her backyard in Woodstock. There, a visitor may come upon a clay mask set among ferns, or a statue decorated with wildflowers and leaves.

Born in London, Mary came to Woodstock after her family recommended the area. She now works in her studio/home along the Beaverkill, which is set among wildflower gardens and tiny lily ponds.

Mary often looks at food from an artist's perspective, and enjoys using pumpkins and zucchinis in her recipes because of their color and texture. She believes that the best cooking pumpkins are found not on area farms, but in New York City's Puerto Rican markets. "I like to use the mottled green and yellow variety," she explains, "the one they call calabash in Mexico, and which has skin that resembles marble." Mary notes that the pumpkins from the Woodstock area are grown for use as jack-o-lanterns and porch decorations rather than for culinary purposes. "Only in a country like America," she observes, "would you cultivate a fruit you don't eat!"

HARVEST TIME SOUP

This recipe was inspired by Mexican food and by the enormous zucchini left in the garden at the end of the growing season. "I don't eschew the larger zucchini for cooking," Mary says. "You can take out the seeds, if you like, but I leave them in."

94

onions, peeled and sliced
vegetable oil
chicken broth
corn scraped from the cob (or use drained, canned corn)
zucchini, cut into cubes (use lots of zucchini, since it provides
 cooking liquid)
tomatoes, cored and quartered
pumpkin, cleaned and cut into chunks
potatoes, peeled and cut into cubes
lime or lemon juice, to taste
hot peppers, cleaned and sliced, if desired
cumin, to taste
coriander, to taste
avocado, peeled and cut into cubes, if desired
soft cheese cut into cubes (Monterey Jack, smoked mozzarella,
 or white cheddar), if desired
toasted sunflower seeds, if desired
plain yogurt, if desired

        In a large pot, sauté onions in small amount of
oil. Add chicken broth, corn, zucchini, tomatoes, pumpkin,
potatoes, citrus juice, peppers, and spices to taste. Bring
to a boil, then reduce and simmer until pumpkin and potatoes
are tender. To serve, place several cubes of avocado in
individual serving bowls. Pour soup over avocado and add
cheese cubes. Or spoon a dollop of yogurt into the soup and
top with toasted sunflower seeds.

Russell Roefs
Santa Claus

"The Christmas Eve Committee surprised me with a biplane."

A resident of Woodstock for over twenty years, Russ has faithfully taken on the role of Santa every Christmas Eve since 1971. Even when he moved to California and flew in for a holiday visit, says Russ, "the Christmas Eve Committee surprised me with a biplane-- **The Spirit of St. Nicholas.** It blew me away." Fortunately, he moved back to Woodstock in time for the next Christmas Eve.

There are always a few thousand people at the village green on Christmas Eve eagerly awaiting the grand entrance of Santa. In past years he has come to town by hot-air balloon, pony-driven sleigh, magic carpet and even by rocketship. But the two most spectacular displays, at least according to Russ, were "when Santa arrived on an elephant and the time he came down from the top of the Dutch Reformed Church steeple by ladder."

Like almost everything in Woodstock, Christmas isn't celebrated in a conventional manner. And Santa might not be considered a conventional guy: Russ is the owner of Consolidated Septic Service, and one of his favorite pastimes is cooking.

NORTH POLE CAJUN SHRIMP

Russ has been cooking for 30 of his 44 years, explaining that as the youngest of eight children, "I had to fend for myself." While stationed in New Mexico with the Army, Russ attended cooking school and he has also studied Western barbecue and Cajun cooking, whence come these hot and fast shrimp for 4.

2 tablespoons oil
2 cloves garlic
3 fresh tomatoes, diced
1 medium size onion, diced
2 large green peppers, diced
1 cup chopped celery
1 cup broth (make this by taking scraps and shells of the peeled
  shrimp and boiling them in two cups of water)
1/2 cup black olives, chopped
red cayenne pepper and salt to taste
1 pound peeled raw shrimp
cooked rice, if desired

In a large covered skillet, sauté garlic, tomatoes and onion in oil; add green pepper and celery. After a few minutes add broth and olives. Sprinkle cayenne pepper and salt over the mixture and add shrimp. Cover and cook for an additional 15 minutes over moderate heat. Serve over rice.

Edith Heckeroth

Heckeroth Plumbing, Electric & Heating

"Adolph hired the future actor, Lee Marvin."

Edith and Adolph Heckeroth have run an essential service business in Woodstock for nearly 45 years and have been married for more than 50 years, an event they celebrated with a trip to Adolph's ancestral home in Germany. They have also had the unusual honor of employing an Academy Award winner as a plumber's assistant. Just after World War II, a Woodstock neighbor, LaMonte Marvin, approached Adolph about employment for his sons, saying, "I have two sons: one wants to write and one wants to be an actor." Edith recalls that "Adolf hired the future actor, Lee Marvin," who won his Oscar for the hilarious role of the drunken gunfighter in **Cat Ballou.** "Lee was a humorous character who enjoyed acting out his exploits as a Marine during the war," says Edith, "and he loved creating sketches about the people he met on his daily rounds as a plumber in the town."

One of Edith's favorite Woodstock traditions is the annual Christmas celebration at the Village Green, when each year, town members and visitors try to guess how Santa Claus will make his appearance. "During the war, a few of us would go out to the green on Christmas Eve and sing carols," she remembers, noting that even in the earliest get-togethers, Santa would arrive in dramatic ways. "One year during a snowstorm, he came by horse and sleigh, another time it was on a small plane that was towed in. Once, they actually lifted Santa up on the steeple of the Dutch Reformed Church and shined a light on him. And darned if you didn't believe in Santa Claus at that moment!"

BETTER BUTTER TARTS

Edith has carefully preserved the family recipes which hail from both Canada and the United States. These tarts come highly recommended by Edith's grandchildren.

98

3/4 cup raisins
hot water
1 cup plus 1 rounded tablespoon brown sugar
1/4 cup butter
1 large egg
1 teaspoon vanilla
2 tablespoons water
dash salt
4 unbaked tart shells

Preheat oven to 375°F. In a small bowl, cover the raisins with hot water and let stand 5 minutes. In a large bowl, cream together the brown sugar and butter; beat in the egg. Stir in vanilla, water and salt. Drain the raisins and stir into batter. Pour batter into unbaked tart shells and bake for 10 minutes or until edges turn brown; lower the oven temperature to 350°F and bake for 15-20 minutes.

EDITH'S BREAD & BUTTER PICKLES

Nothing is better with a picnic or barbecue than crunchy, spicy-sweet pickles. These are easy to make and the quantity per batch is only 6 pints.

In a large kettle, mix together the following:

1 pound light brown sugar
2 tablespoons mustard seed
3 tablespoons salt
1 teaspoon celery seed
1 teaspoon turmeric
3 cups vinegar

Slice and add:

9 large cucumbers
2 large green peppers, cored and seeded
4 large onions, peeled

Bring mixture to a boil over moderately high heat, stirring frequently from the bottom of the kettle to the top. Pour into sterilized jars and seal according to manufacturer's directions.

CLEAR THE PIPES CHILI SAUCE

This chili sauce is one of Edith's specialties, which she prepares each year at harvest time.

Wash, peel and quarter:
    1 peck of tomatoes (about 12 1/2 pounds)

Put through food grinder or chop fine:
    6 green peppers, cored and seeded
    1 tablespoon crushed red pepper
    6 large white onions, peeled

To the above mixture, add:
    tomatoes
    2 cups brown sugar
    3 cups cider vinegar
    3 tablespoons coarse salt
    1 tablespoon black pepper
    1 tablespoon allspice
    1 teaspoon ground cloves
    1 tablespoon ginger
    1 tablespoon cinnamon
    1 tablespoon nutmeg
    1 tablespoon celery seed

Put ingredients into a large kettle and simmer slowly until thickened, about 4 hours; stir frequently to prevent scorching. Pour sauce into sterilized jars and seal according to manufacturer's directions. Makes about 4 1/2 quarts.

Fran Breitkopf
realtor

"I ended up in real estate at the right time."

Of her early days in Woodstock, Fran vividly remembers the town just before the '69 Festival. "Woodstock was closed," she recalls. "The merchants wanted to board up their windows, they were so afraid of the crowds. There was even a sign erected on the highway near the entrance to Woodstock that read 'THE FESTIVAL IS NOT HERE'." Despite these efforts, a sort of anti-promotion, people still flocked to the town and ended up sleeping on the lawns and hanging out on the Village Green.

A former teacher, Fran came to Woodstock from New York City and ended up dropping out of the school system and selling real estate. She eventually opened Teran Real Estate on Mill Hill Road, and with the recent boom in Woodstock real estate, she doesn't have much time for everyday cooking. Holidays and weekends are Fran's time for using recipes whipped up from her family cookbooks, and "a little imagination and expediency."

ONE POT CABBAGE SOUP & STUFFED CABBAGE

This recipe came from her Russian grandmother, who was, remembers Fran, "a great cook-- she always did everything by taste, no specific measurements or cooking times." This is an unusual one-pot meal, richer than a plain soup, more satisfying than just stuffed cabbage. True to Grandma's spirit, you'll have to taste and taste again to make this recipe work.

"Wash cabbage in hot water (so that the leaves will come apart.) Remove large leaves (save for stuffing) and chop the small leaves into fairly large-sized pieces. Rub a little salt through the chopped leaves. Put a lot of water and a large can of tomato puree in a large pot and boil them with the cabbage. Taste so it won't be salty, put in some citric acid (or lemon juice) and taste to see that it's not too sour; add some sugar and taste again. To make stuffing, dissolve sour salt (or citric acid or lemon juice) and some sugar in water. Add this to ground round or a ground chuck blend. Fill large cabbage leaves with chopped meat mixture and put into soup. Cook until the cabbage leaves are soft; the soup is done."

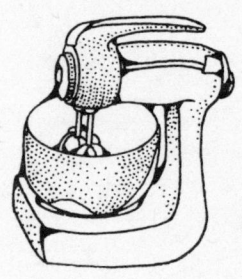

HONEY YOGURT CHEESECAKE

Fran devised this recipe while trying to create a lower-in-cholesterol cheesecake. It's lighter and a little more tart than traditional treats of this type.

Crust

1 1/4 cups graham cracker crumbs (crush the crackers between
   two sheets of wax paper or whirl crackers in blender)
4 tablespoons sifted superfine or confectioners sugar
6 tablespoons melted butter
1 teaspoon cinnamon
1/4 teaspoon nutmeg

Mix together ingredients and pat into springform pan.

Filling

2 8-ounce packages cream cheese
1 cup sugar
1 cup plain yogurt
1 1/2 teaspoons vanilla flavoring
1 1/2 teaspoons almond flavoring
3 eggs
1 graham cracker crust in springform pan

Topping

1/2 teaspoon vanilla
2 teaspoons honey
1/2 cup yogurt

Preheat oven to 350°F. For filling, cream together cream cheese, sugar, yogurt and flavorings; add the eggs, one at a time. Pour mixture into prepared crust, making certain batter does not touch the top edge of the pan. Bake for 50 minutes, or until a crack appears on cake's surface; remove cake from oven, but close oven door to keep heat inside. For topping, mix together vanilla, honey and yogurt. Spoon gently onto top of cake. Return cake to oven for 5 minutes. Cool at room temperature, then chill and serve.

Susun Weed

herbalist/green witch

"I speak for the earth, I speak for the wild and virgin things."

Those who meet Susun soon realize that the stereotype of an elderly woman who conjures up the devil is far from what witches are, or ever were. What's a green witch? According to Susun, witches are herbalists, midwives and healers who nurture the healing powers implicit in us all. She laughs, "I'm a green witch-- green is for the plants." We were greeted in Susun's driveway by Cous-cous, her gregarious pet goose. "He'll protect your car from the goats," Susun assured us, as she led the way through her gardens. The house blossoms, both inside and out, with fresh and dried herbs, flowers and weeds, as befits a woman who considers herself a green witch.

Susun's interest in herbs took root elsewhere, but Woodstock is where it flowered and she is completely self-taught. "I'm continually learning new things about herbs," she says. "Everyone knows something about plants, so I learn from the earth, the plants and all I meet." Of her unusual name, Susun explains that "Weed is indeed my name, although not my father's or my ex-husband's. I speak for the earth, I speak for the wild and virgin things, I speak for the weeds."

In 1978, Susun established the Wise Woman Center. "It's my home," she explained, "a sacred and safe place for women, a homestead and workshop center." During our visit we met two green witch apprentices, one from New Mexico and the other from Toronto; they had just milked the goats and were about to make cheese. One-day workshops such as "Talking with Plants" are open to all while apprenticeships and longer workshops are for women only.

Susun took us on a "Weed Walk" through her extensive gardens to collect the weeds and greens and as we ambled, she offered tastes of an amazing array of aromatic, flavorful leaves, seeds and flowers and explained the medicinal as well as the culinary uses of each one. "Smell this," she said, handing us a stalk of fragrant lovage, "it's reputed to renew one's interest in life." But clearly, this is one herb that Susun Weed does not need!

SUSUN'S GREEN WITCH SALAD

Pick small amounts of each green. Rinse only if necessary, tear into small pieces, and serve with a dressing made of olive oil, herb vinegar, tamari and garlic powder. Remember, you won't need to add herbs to the dressing.

wood sorrel (good source of Vitamin C)
lamb's quarter (good source of calcium)
chickweed (spring green)
violet leaves (a reputed cancer preventive)
yellow dock (excellent source of iron)
cat-mint (also known as catnip; just a touch, it's very strong)
bee balm (also known as bergamot; either red or purple, although the purple tastes better than any commercial oregano)
shepherd's purse
Queen Anne's lace blossoms
red clover blossoms
plantain
wild pepper
lettuce (optional!)

Become accustomed to eating and creating a foraged salad by making a conventional salad and adding new weeds and herbs each time you prepare it. The foraged salad will change throughout the year, since different greens are available every month. As you discover your favorite herbs and weeds, you'll develop a cycle of salads for the seasons. **CAUTION**: Do not use any mushroom or plant until you are certain of what it is. Check several field guides (or take a workshop with Susun.)

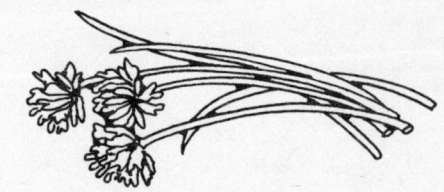

WISE WOMAN NETTLE TEA

One of Susun's "ally" herbs is the stinging nettle, which she says is "a powerful blood and kidney building herb, rich in a wide variety of nutrients, including iron, calcium, vitamins E, K, A, C, and D, chlorophyll, amino acids and trace minerals." Susun prepares the brew as follows:

Pick the nettles in the spring (be certain to wear gloves.) Dry nettles in a breezy, dark place, then store in a paper bag. To make the brew, put a handful of the dried nettles in a teapot or jar, and pour on boiling water to fill the container. Cover tightly and allow to steep overnight. The next day, strain and serve the tea warm or cold. Susun believes that since it takes several hours for the minerals to move into the water from the nettles, this method is the best for extracting all the nourishment from the plant.

Terrin & Hal Levitt
potter & playwright

"We felt we had lived here in a previous life."

"For 42 years I did the cooking," laughs Terrin, "and for the past few years Hal has taken over in the kitchen." Hal explains: "I started out with what a lot of schnooks my age begin with-- Chinese and Japanese cuisine, because it's easy."

A former drama professor at Hunter College, Hal is the author of off-Broadway plays including **An Acting Family, The Passion of Gross** and **One Foot to the Sea,** which won the award for best off-Broadway production of 1953. He is also known for two plays of local interest, **Picnic at the Little Bear** and **Woodstock Chronicles,** a play which tells the story of the town through history and legend. Terrin's pottery, which is characterized by a rare crystalline glaze, is well known to collectors of modern ceramics and is represented in many fine stores and galleries throughout the United States.

The Levitts moved to Woodstock in 1974. "We were driving into town to visit friends," explains Terrin, "when we saw the Playhouse, which Hal loved, and the craft shops, which I loved, and we felt at home immediately, like we had lived here in a previous life. Within 20 minutes of our arrival, we bought a weekend cottage." Now permanent residents, Terrin and Hal live in a 19th-century building that also houses their studios, and was home to Hervey White, Carl Eric Linden and other artists during the the construction of the Byrdcliffe Arts Colony.

COLORFUL CAVIAR PIE

"You can get this dish ready in ten minutes," says Terrin. "And what's nice is that the colors, which are red or black, yellow and green, can be varied to fit the season or the occasion." If any of the pie is left over, shape it into a log, wrap it in waxed paper and store in the refrigerator. Or simply use it to stuff hard-boiled eggs.

1 8-ounce package cream cheese
4 tablespoons sour cream
2 tablespoons dried onion
small jar red or black caviar
1 hard-boiled egg, pressed through a sieve or sliced
1 tablespoon chopped parsley
3 chopped scallions

Mix cream cheese, sour cream and onion together. Spread on bottom and sides of 10" pie pan. Spoon caviar into the center of the cheese "pie." Arrange egg around the caviar, trim the borders of the pie with parsley and scallions. Serve with crackers or pumpernickel bread.

UPSIDE DOWN CHICKEN

Hal insists that the chicken must be fried skin side down so the bird cooks in its own fat.

2 1/2 - 3 pounds chicken, cut into pieces (do not remove skin)
3 tablespoons butter
salt and pepper to taste
2 garlic cloves, unpeeled
1/2 teaspoon thyme
1 bay leaf
1/4 cup white wine
1/3 cup water
buttered noodles, if desired

Gash the chicken legs for easier cooking. Using a heavy skillet, melt the butter, add salt and pepper to taste, and lay the chicken in, skin side down. Over medium high heat, sauté the chicken for 5 minutes, turning once. Add garlic, thyme and bay leaf; turn chicken skin side down, cover, reduce heat and cook for 15 minutes. Remove chicken to warm platter. To the remaining fat in pan, add wine and water, and simmer at low heat, until liquid is reduced by half. Serve chicken over buttered noodles, and pour wine sauce over all.

PLAYWRIGHT'S PORK CHOPS ORIENTAL

Hal got this recipe "from a Chinese gentleman, who was amazed at the American interpretation of Chinese food." This, according to Hal, is the real thing.

Marinade

1 tablespoon light soy sauce
1 tablespoon dark soy sauce
1 tablespoon dry sherry
2 teaspoons sesame oil
1 teaspoon sugar
1/8 teaspoon white pepper
2 tablespoons cornstarch

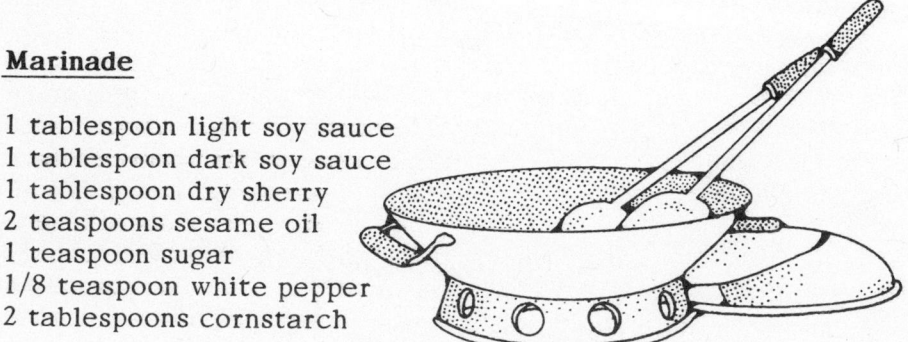

Whisk all ingredients together and set aside.

Pork Chops

Six 3/8" center cut pork chops
marinade
vegetable oil
large onion, cut into strips
3 tablespoons chicken stock
salt to taste

Cut away all fat and bone from the chops. Using a blunt cleaver, lightly pound both sides of chops. In a large pan, arrange chops in one layer. Pour marinade over chops and marinate each side of pork chops for 15 minutes. Heat oil in wok or pan, arrange chops in pan and increase heat to medium high. Brown both sides of pork; cook pork until done and remove to heated platter. Add onion to wok or pan; increase heat to high, add stock and salt to taste. Cook onion until moisture is evaporated. Arrange onion strips around pork on platter and serve.

Steve Charney & Harry
ventriloquist & friend

"He seems to thrive on the ridiculous."

Although Harry can be found during working hours perched on Steve's knee, at home he is as relaxed as any three foot wooden ventriloquist's dummy can be. Attired in a Hawaiian print shirt and Bermuda shorts, Harry introduced us to his "assistant" Steve, who didn't become second banana overnight.

While Harry went off to get coffee, Queens-born Steve explains his quest for fame: "I was always the class clown and wanted to be an actor, a star. But I discovered I was a ham instead, and I didn't have the patience to go to auditions." So Steve ended up studying photography in college and after a couple of years living in different places, ended up in Woodstock, where he had friends. It was "love at first sight, a town run by hippies, people like me," he says, recalling his first impression of Woodstock in the 1970s.

Steve sort of backed into the local entertainment scene. One day a friend saw him performing some silly songs and magic tricks, and asked Steve to appear at a nephew's birthday party. "When I got paid," Steve recalls, "I looked at the money and thought, 'Wow, this is great, I can actually make a living like this!'"

Woodstock's radio station WDST went into operation on April 29, 1980 (before that, one of the most famous music communities in the country had no radio station of its own.) "The Steve Show" starring Steve Charney, went on the air days later, a mixture of music, talk, and audio effects, which included Steve dressing in a gorilla suit or painting his toenails green. A **New Yorker** "Profile" once described Steve Charney as "someone who does not shrink from puns, riddles, tongue twisters, knock-knock jokes or well-aged humor. He seems to thrive on the ridiculous."

The weekly show soon had a faithful following which kept Steve on a constant lookout for material. After reading a book on ventriloquism, he found a routine that featured a dummy. Steve tried showcasing the voice of a character called Harry on the air and in one routine, Steve got sick and couldn't make it, so Harry took over. The voice became so popular that it needed a body (for live appearances like parties) and Harry was born. Now the two are business partners, combining Steve's talent and Harry's charisma.

Asked to discuss their combined culinary talents, Harry bursts into song. We can't say much for the lyrics-- neither can Steve-- but Harry, as usual, had the last word.

Harry's Song

Monday we get bread and water,
Tuesday we get water and bread.
Wednesday we get bread and water,
Thursday we get water and bread.
Friday we complain to the kitchen,
Saturday the kitchen complains to the head.
Sunday we get something different,
We get water...without the bread.

HARRY'S PB & B

After Steve explained that the most difficult letters for a ventriloquist to articulate are P and B, we understood why Harry loves the following treat and recommends it for kids. The recipe was passed on to Steve by a fat babysitter from his childhood.

1 banana
your favorite brand of peanut butter

Slice the banana lengthwise. Generously spread peanut butter over one piece. Make a sandwich by adding the top banana and enjoy with friends.

CHILI CON CHARNEY

Not to be outdone, Steve gave us the following recipe for what he calls the best chili ever.

3 tablespoons butter or olive oil
1 large onion, minced
2 cloves garlic
1 pound chopped beef
3 cups water
1 1/3 cups chopped tomatoes
1 green pepper, minced
1/2 teaspoon celery seed
1/4 teaspoon cayenne pepper
1 teaspoon cumin seed, crushed
1 small bay leaf
2 tablespoons chili powder
1/8 teaspoon basil
1 1/2 teaspoon salt
1 can kidney beans, if desired

Heat the butter in a skillet, add onion and garlic and sauté until lightly browned; add meat and brown. Transfer the mixture to a large saucepan and add the remaining ingredients except the kidney beans. Bring to a boil, reduce heat and simmer uncovered until sauce is thickened (about 2 hours.) Just before serving, add kidney beans.

KNOCK ON WOOD MOZZARELLA CHUNKS

Steve discovered this recipe at the Italian Market in Philadelphia.

1 pound mozzarella, cut into 1" cubes
1 cup olive oil
2 tablespoons freshly chopped basil **OR**
 1 tablespoon dried basil
1 teaspoon red pepper
2 teaspoons oregano
2 cloves of garlic, finely chopped
1/2 teaspoon salt, if desired

In a large bowl, stir together all ingredients except mozzarella until well blended. Add mozzarella, and marinate overnight in refrigerator. Serve at room temperature.

DANDY BRANDY PIE

Elise Glenne, Harry & Steve's friend, gave us this dessert recipe, one of Steve's favorites (Harry prefers peanut butter.)

1 envelope unflavored gelatin
1/2 cup cold water
2/3 cup sugar
1/4 teaspoon salt
3 eggs yolks
3 egg whites
1/4 cup cognac
1/4 cup creme de cacao
2 cups heavy cream, whipped
9" chocolate graham cracker crust
mini-chocolate chips, for garnish
chopped pecans or walnuts, for garnish

In a saucepan, sprinkle gelatin over cold water. Add half the sugar, the salt and egg yolks; stir to blend. Heat the mixture slowly, stirring constantly, until the gelatin dissolves and the mixture thickens. Do not boil. Remove from heat and stir in cognac and creme de cacao. Chill for 15 minutes. Beat egg whites until stiff, then gradually beat in the remaining sugar and fold into thickened mixture. Fold in half of the whipped cream. Pour into crust and chill for several hours. Garnish with remaining whipped cream, and sprinkle pie with chocolate chips and nuts, if desired.

Milton Glaser
graphic designer

"Our friends had a barn, and we slept in the corn crib."

Graphic design is everywhere, but few graphic artists command the instant recognition that belongs to Milton Glaser. A founder of **New York Magazine,** he also designed the Grand Union and I LOVE NEW YORK logos, as well as posters of such diverse subjects as Bob Dylan and the Catskills.

What is it about this region that offers Milton inspiration? Just what is so magical and enchanting in these hills? "There is an extraordinary range of landscapes in the Catskills," he says. "It's a true wilderness, unlike Europe, where almost every inch is cultivated." Milton and his wife, Shirley, have owned their Woodstock home for more than 25 years, but their first visits with friends were a shade less comfortable. "Our friends had a barn," laughs Milton, in recalling the weekend visits, "and we slept in the corn crib."

Now friends who stop by the Glaser home are likely to be invited to try some fabulous food. "Northern Italian is our favorite," says Milton without hesitation. "We often make risotto, pasta, stews or soups if we're having guests." Although he likes food to be well presented when he dines out, Milton doesn't think too much of the nouvelle cuisine, where "there are three little artichokes and two string beans on a plate." That kind of presentation, "where the sense of artifice is apparent," isn't his style. Color and substance are his keywords, whether in posters or at the table.

DIVINE DEVILED CHICKEN

Milton describes Shirley as "a wonderful cook" and this recipe is one of their summer favorites. Milton suggests serving the chicken at room temperature to get the fullest flavor. The Glasers usually accompany this dish with a string bean salad and tomatoes drizzled with olive oil and basil.

1 whole chicken
1 lemon
1/4 cup olive oil
1/2 teaspoon salt
1/2 teaspoon oregano
1/2 teaspoon thyme
1/2 teaspoon basil
1 tablespoon coarse black pepper

   Wash the chicken, remove the backbone and flatten it out. Rub chicken with halved lemon and paint with olive oil. In a mortar, pulverize the salt, oregano, thyme, basil and pepper. "Use lots of pepper," advises Milton; "that's the key to this recipe." Dust the chicken with the dried herb mixture until it is completely covered. Bake for 45 minutes at 350°F or until done.

Jane & Joe Veillette

two-fifths of The Phantoms

"Woodstock is a place...that still has a little city vibe to it."

Both Jane and Joe are members of The Phantoms, a popular Woodstock rock and roll group whose first album, "THE PHANTOMS!" was mixed at Bearsville Studios and released in 1987. Even daughter Jasmine ("she came really close to being a Willow, but my mother had a fit when she heard the name") has been part of the Phantoms' act.

One of their most nerve-wracking performances came at Radio City Music Hall. Jane recalls looking out at 5,000 do-wop fans who were there to hear groups like the Capris. The Phantoms were one of the opening bands, new to the Hall, and their lead singer was suffering from a bad case of laryngitis. Jane laughs, as she recalls the night, "My lips were quivering so much I was afraid that I wouldn't be able to get the first line of the song out. Then we started to sing, and the audience loved it."

The Brooklyn/Bronx couple headed to Woodstock because, according to Jane, "It's a place away from New York City that still has a little city vibe to it." They were convinced they needed at least a small shot of urban-ity after living in Grahamsville and discovering that their neighbors, who had been there for forty years, were still called the "people from Long Island."

When the subject turned to favorite foods, Joe said, "If you asked me a year ago, I'd have to say cheeseburgers were right up there, but now, simple vegetarian dishes with rice or kasha are more satisfying to me." Jane is a fan of fruit salads, and both of them enthusiastically jotted down their favorite recipes.

JANE'S DO-WOP BEAN DIP

Some of the Veillette's closest friends started out as fans. In fact, this dish was passed along from a fan to Jane, who added her own harmonies.

1 can refried beans
1/2 packet of your favorite taco seasoning mix
2 medium avocados, chopped
8 ounces sour cream
2 medium tomatoes, chopped
1 small onion, finely chopped
1/2 cup shredded jalapeño cheese
taco chips

Mix the beans and taco seasoning and spread evenly over a 9" pan. Sprinkle avocados on top of the beans. Spread sour cream over avocados. Sprinkle tomatoes, onion and cheese over mixture; pack down lightly. Serve at room temperature with taco chips.

JOE'S ORGANICALLY DERIVED DRESSING

Joe doesn't do much cooking these days, but when he does, one of his specialties is this dressing. Of its origin, Joe states, "I wanted to make Russian dressing one day using ketchup and mayonnaise, but I ran out of ketchup and used mustard instead."

1/4 cup vegetable oil
1/2 cup mayonnaise
1/3 cup Dijon mustard
1 tablespoon barbecue sauce
1 teaspoon parsley flakes
1/4 cup mashed avocado, if desired
1 teaspoon curry powder, if desired

In a small bowl or jar, mix all ingredients together and blend thoroughly. Store leftover dressing in the refrigerator.

Aileen Cramer
activist

"Two artists in the family were quite enough."

Daughter of two renowned artists, Konrad Cramer and Florence Ballin, Aileen grew up in Woodstock during the height of its artist colony days. "I went to the Little Red Schoolhouse, which had one room and eight grades," she says, but in retrospect, the real fun came from attending the Maverick festivals.

"Those summers in Woodstock were wonderful; there was a very bohemian atmosphere," she recalls. "We went to the Maverick early in the afternoon; in those days, the festivals were held near today's concert hall. It was wild. There would be campfires, drinking and dancing, which could go on for 24 hours, and sometimes, we went in costume. One summer the artists built a full-sized merry-go-round and another year they constructed treehouses. I remember one man had too much to drink, and rolled right out of his treehouse and into our campfire." Aileen notes that the communities of artists and native Woodstockians got along fairly well. "It's true we didn't talk about many of the same things," she laughs, "but then most of the farmers were not interested in discussing the work of Picasso."

Following her Woodstock childhood, Aileen worked in the theater as an actress and puppeteer, and eventually became active in the Women's International League for Peace and Freedom, one of the oldest peace movements in the country. Now, back living in the gracious home she inherited from her parents, Aileen serves on the Woodstock Town Board and the board of the Woodstock Artists Association. Although she once studied art with Kuniyoshi and was considered a talented painter, she's philosophical about her career choices: "two artists in the family were quite enough!"

POOR WOMAN'S PASTA

Once concerned with low-cost meals, Aileen is now cholesterol conscious, and recommends this recipe on both counts. The yogurt adds pizazz.

2 small zucchini, sliced
1/4 cup vegetable oil
1 teaspoon sugar
2 cloves garlic
1/2 cup plain yogurt
1/4 cup grated parmesan cheese
1 pound cooked fettuccine

Sauté the zucchini in vegetable oil. When soft, sprinkle a little sugar over it. Squeeze garlic juice over fettuccine and stir in yogurt. Spoon zucchini over pasta, and sprinkle with parmesan cheese.

Phyllis Engelmyer
yoga instructor

"I learned to cook in self-defense."

Her father is from Israel, her mother was born in Russia and she grew up in Brooklyn, so we asked Phyllis what she considered traditional home cooking. "My mother worshipped Fifties culture," she remembers, "plastic dishes and tv dinners. And my Russian grandmother would first boil, then broil, meat to death. I learned to cook in self-defense."

Phyllis began studying yoga at the age of 18, both in India and Japan. She also followed in the footsteps of her Russian grandfather, a pushcart salesman who regularly traveled with his buttons and zippers from Kiev to Outer Mongolia. For several years, Phyllis's wares consisted of exotic kushi cloth, a lovely, handstamped fabric from Afghanistan. "But with the revolution there," she says, "the world stopped for me. My husband and I even had a difficult time getting out of the country."

Today, Phyllis teaches daily yoga classes and cooks part-time at the Tibetan monastery. A vegetarian who extols the effects yoga has on the body, she does not consume any sugar, caffeine, or white flour. "Sugar creates an unnatural blockage in the body," claims Phyllis. "To maintain a balanced diet, I eat whole grains, root and green vegetables, beans and cheese on occasion." About hatha yoga, for more than 20 years an integral part of her life, Phyllis says, "I practice the physical postures twice each day. Staying in shape is like working to keep a musical instrument in tune."

MY GRANDFATHER'S MUSHROOM BARLEY SOUP

"This is actually my Russian grandfather's recipe;

I often make it at the monastery during the winter months. It freezes nicely, and can be made into a vegetable loaf as well."

1/2 cup dried lima beans (or any type of beans)
vegetable oil
1 large onion, peeled and diced
2 carrots or parsnips, peeled and cubed
2 stalks celery, chopped
1/2 pound sliced mushrooms
1 green pepper, cored and sliced
3 cloves garlic, pressed
1/2 cup barley
salt and pepper
8 cups water

Soak the lima beans overnight; drain. In a large pot, heat oil and saute the onion, carrots, celery, mushrooms, green pepper and garlic. Stir in the barley and lima beans. Add salt and pepper to taste. Add water, and bring to boil, then reduce heat and simmer until barley is tender, approximately 30 minutes. To make a vegetable loaf, cook beans and barley according to package directions, add remaining ingredients (except the water), press the vegetables into an oiled loaf pan and bake at 350°F for 30 minutes.

Frank & Linda Luther
bassist & baker

"My 36-hour spaghetti sauce comes out different every time."

Hearing bassist Frank Luther today, no one would believe that it took him a year to coax some recognizable sounds from the unwieldy instrument (his first song was "Taps".) But his innate talent, determination and good humor have made him into one of the best jazz bassists in the business.

Frank grew up on the west side of Chicago and studied the bass in school primarily to get out of homeroom. His first choice of an instrument was the trumpet, but since he would have to buy one and the family was short on cash, that was ruled out. His second choice was drums, but the percussion section had too many members. "I was very tall, even then," Frank laughs, "so my music teacher talked me into trying the bass; no one else wanted to play it."

Frank met his wife, Linda, a Columbus, Ohio native, at **Gregory's**, an Upper East Side Manhattan jazz club. She was working as a Pan Am flight attendant, and like Frank, she was living in the city. It wasn't long before they bought a house in Woodstock, spent weekends renovating it and finally, moved up permanently. For a while, Linda says, "Frank would go off to play and I would go off to fly," but after their son was born, Linda started a special order baking service while Frank still commutes to gigs in New York City.

Frank and Linda both enjoy cooking, his specialty being Thirty-Six-Hour Spaghetti Sauce into which "pork, chicken, whole tomatoes and whatever you have in the house" are mixed. "It comes out different every time," says Frank. "The important thing is to simmer the sauce for several hours...it's like transitions in a musical composition." Frank maintains that anyone can make his sauce. "I can't give you the recipe; you have to make it up as you go along," he explains. Like any good jazz composition, the sauce is mostly improvisation.

FIFTEEN MINUTE TROUT

In contrast to the Thirty-Six Hour Sauce, Linda gave us one of her favorite fast fish recipes. The trout usually come from the Grand Union if one of the local streams doesn't pan out.

4 whole trout
olive oil
1/4 cup tamari
juice of 1/2 lemon
2 cloves garlic, crushed

Rub trout with olive oil. Prepare a marinade with the remaining ingredients and marinate trout for 1 hour. Sauté in large frying pan for 15-20 minutes, or grill over a fire for 20 minutes.

BASS-IC ZUCCHINI BREAD

Linda's specialties are desserts, and here's one the family enjoys.

3 eggs
3/4 cup honey
1 cup oil
2 1/2 cups grated zucchini
1 teaspoon vanilla
3 1/2 cups flour (measure after sifting)
3 teaspoons cinnamon
1 teaspoon nutmeg
1/2 teaspoon ground cloves
1 teaspoon baking powder
1 teaspoon baking soda
1 cup walnuts
1 cup raisins

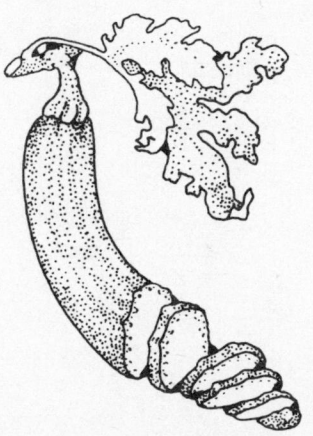

Preheat oven to 350°F. In a large bowl, mix together eggs, honey and oil; stir in zucchini and vanilla. In a separate bowl, sift together the flour, spices, baking powder and baking soda; stir into the zucchini mixture. Mix in nuts and raisins. Bake in a large greased loaf pan for 1 hour.

Jeff & Jane Brody
attorney & journalist

"My favorite foods, which I absolutely adore, are salad and bread!"

Most people know Jane from her **New York Times** column and her health and nutrition books. "I take no vitamins," says Jane, "since I believe that all the beneficial effects of vitamins are obtained directly through foods, not supplements." Eating well is the best way to go, according to Jane, who has degrees in biochemistry and science writing. Brooklyn-born Jane still resides in that borough, occasionally weekending at her home in Woodstock, which she bought in 1981 with her brother, Jeffrey, a year-round resident and matrimonial attorney.

The Brodys' interest in healthful eating has deep roots. After their mother died while Jeff and Jane were teenagers, their father took over the household's management. "He had a natural instinct for fresh fruits, vegetables and grains," recalls Jane. "We had fresh fruit year round, whole wheat flour in our pancakes and yogurt before almost anyone even knew what it was." Jeff concurs. "My father taught me how to shop; grocery shopping was one of his favorite activities," he says. "My father must have died happy; he was food shopping at Waldbaum's when he went."

Jane's husband, Richard Engquist, a lyricist and writer, shares the cooking at home. "In our house we don't throw any food away. My husband has a talent for leftovers...he can throw a few things from the fridge together and the dish always tastes better than the original." Richard taught Jane about soups as well as how to bake bread, which "he learned at his grandmother's elbow growing up in Minnesota." Jane says, "My favorite foods, which I absolutely adore, are salad and bread." Once Jane gave up bread for two days. "And on the third day I dreamed about bagels." She stopped buying bagels last year, however, when her twin sons went off to college. "Otherwise, I'd have a bagel on each thigh!" For years, Jane baked most of the bread consumed by her family. "I'd get the dough ready by 6:30 a.m.," she explained, "then I'd go biking and the dough would rise."

124

For Jane, the most difficult part about writing cookbooks is getting down the exact amounts of ingredients. "I still do the 'pot throwing trick,'" she says, explaining that this is how she cooks at home. Jeffrey elaborated on the technique, which includes adding to the pot as you go along: "I smell a spice, and think if it would taste good in the dish I'm preparing," he says. "I have the basic concept in mind, but the dish always varies and I enjoy anticipating the nuances of the new creation, which are always different from the last time I made the dish."

Jane emphasizes that cooking from scratch isn't difficult. "When I cook, I make double batches of everything and freeze half of it. Very rarely does anyone have to rely on frozen or fast foods-- they're not always faster!"

JANE BRODY'S ANTI-CANCER SOUP

The name of this soup comes from the fact that it contains cabbage and carrots, both cancer-fighting vegetables, according to Jane. She buys fresh, raw turkey at the Grand Union in Woodstock. "It takes about 15 minutes to throw everything into the pot," she says. The only disadvantage to this recipe is that canned tomato juice has a good amount of sodium. Jane suggests using unsalted tomato juice or fresh tomatoes if that is a concern.

1 pound ground turkey
1 large Spanish onion, chopped
1 48-ounce can of tomato juice
1 small head of cabbage, chopped (approximately 1 1/4 pounds)
3 large carrots, diced
3 stalks of celery, diced
freshly ground pepper to taste
water, if needed, depending upon the consistency desired

In a non-stick pot, scramble the turkey with the onion and cook until turkey is lightly browned. Drain off any excess fat that cooks out. Add tomato juice, cabbage, carrots and celery. Bring to a boil. Reduce heat; cover and simmer for about 1 1/2 hours. If soup is too thick, add water. Season with pepper. Serves 6-8 people.

125

THE OTHER BRODY'S SALMON SOAK

Jeff has enjoyed fishing for the past 20 years, and he keeps a rowboat at the Ashokan Reservoir for weekend use. "Nothing is more beautiful than watching the sunset there," he says. He also travels to Lake Ontario to fish for salmon, and he can produce a photograph of himself with a 27-pound fish. "I still have him in the freezer," Jeff laughs. "I certainly don't go to a restaurant and order salmon; I came back from that trip with 180 pounds of it."

Jeff enjoys fish cooked so that the middle remains moist. "A marinade, in essence, pre-cooks the fish so that you can keep the center rare when it is grilled." Jeff grills fish year round and this is his famous marinade. "Almost nothing," in his opinion, should be "prepared without some enhancement."

white wine Worcestershire sauce
sherry
white wine
rice or wine vinegar ("If I'm feeling yuppie, I'll use balsamic
  vinegar.")
gingery soy sauce
fresh ginger, grated
fresh parsley, chopped
fresh dill ("If I have it.")
honey, to taste

Mix everything together according to taste and let the fish soak at least one hour. Jeff never uses salt, but advises: "If you over-sour the marinade with vinegar and it's too tart, add some honey. This will cut the acid."

COMPOST COMPOTE

Jeffrey called his sister one day to find out how to prepare a "compost." Richard answered the telephone and began explaining how to get the garden mixture going. When Richard mentioned the addition of manure, Jeffrey said what he meant was a fruit compote. Jeff notes that the addition of quince will counteract some of the sweetness and add a nice tart flavor.

dried apricots
raisins
currants
large pitted prunes
one or two sliced lemons
fresh ground coriander
nutmeg
apple cider (you may substitute water)
sweet/tart apples, peeled and sliced
Devoe pears, peeled and sliced
one or two quince, if desired
Napoleon   brandy
red wine, if desired

In a large, thick-bottomed stew pot, cook the apricots, raisins, currants, prunes and lemons with coriander and nutmeg on low heat. Use a little water or apple cider as a liquid base. Cook until the fruit gets soft but is still intact. (Some of the fruits, like prunes, will break up; raisins and apricots will stay whole.) Add the apples, pears, quince, more water or cider, and some brandy and wine. Stir in additional coriander and nutmeg and cook until the pears and apples soften. Serve warm or chilled, but the compote, says Jeff, gets better with age.

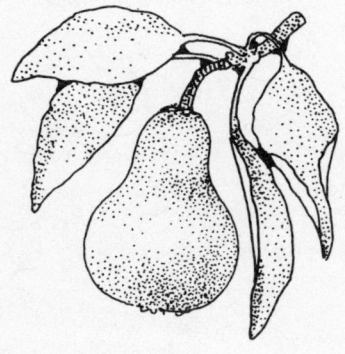

Chip (Clifford) Chase
backhoe operator, Woodstock dump

"I've had blisters on my hands from all the mixing."

Although he has been a member of the Lake Hill volunteer fire department since the 1950s, it is only in the past few years that Chip has been running their Sunday pancake breakfasts. The tradition began, according to Chip, when the men decided to "do something nice" for the Ladies Auxiliary one Easter Sunday and ended up cooking breakfast on campstoves for more than 80 people. The men realized that the breakfast could be used as a regular fundraiser, and now they are held every third Sunday of the month, September through May, from 8 - 11 a.m. at the firehouse.

The day of a firehouse breakfast begins at 5 a.m. for Chip and his crew, since breakfast consists not only of pancakes, but of scrambled eggs, sausages and coffee as well. "The batter is all hand-stirred, and I've had blisters on my hands from all the mixing," says Chip. The crew even boasts a professional or two, Chip explains, noting that "Our grill man used to be a short-order cook...and boy, can he put'em off the grill!" Holidays usually mean a few surprises at the breakfasts. St. Patrick's Day may reveal some kelly green pancakes and at Christmas, Santa has been known to show up in a horse and buggy.

A native of Brown Station on the south side of the Ashokan Reservoir, Chip learned to cook in home economics class, which he took, he says, "because of all the good-looking girls." He's a purist with it comes to making pancakes. "I like mine thin, not thick," he says. "Some firehouses make'em thick and add vanilla to the batter, but I don't." But all is not hard work at the firehouse. Laughing, Chip told us about his "biscuit and gravy award," a petrified cow-pat, that was presented as a sort of "thank you" for all his work. "It's even framed," he says. "We work hard there, but we also have a lot of fun."

LAKE HILL PANCAKES FOR COMPANY

Even though the following recipe may make a couple of hundred or more pancakes, you can reduce it to suit your needs by following package directions. But Chip warns that you have to remember a couple of things, no matter how many pancakes you make. One, oil your grill or pan once with vegetable oil and then forget about it. Two, use milk, not water, to thin the batter. Three, serve with lots of butter, maple syrup and as much sausage as you can eat.

4-pound box Aunt Jemima's Pancake Mix
1 gallon milk
13 eggs
1/2 cup oil

Mix the above ingredients (remember, by hand only!) Cook on a hot grill, and if you are a member of the fire department, you're sure to raise some dough.

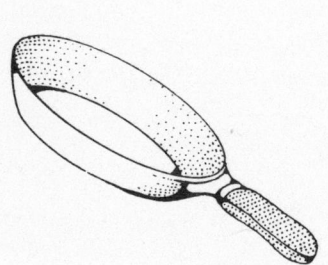

Eduardo Chavez
artist

"I still cook by instinct."

Full-time painter and sculptor Ed Chavez's work is found in the collections of the Museum of Modern Art, the Hirschhorn and the Library of Congress, and his art has been featured in publications such as **Time, Life,** and **The New Yorker.**

Ed began painting with the Federal W.P.A. program in 1936, specializing in large murals that depict America's Western heritage. He spent a summer studying with Arnold Blanch, who urged him to settle in Woodstock after a stint in the Armed Forces, and Ed has been a Woodstockian since 1945.

Born in New Mexico and raised in Colorado, Ed was the only child in his family of 11 brothers and sisters who enjoyed watching his mother cook. "In New Mexico, they measure in a handful of this or that," he says. "The only difference is that you might add a large handful or a small one." This was the way Ed's mother taught him to measure ingredients, and he says, "I still cook by instinct. Even when I use a cookbook, I add my own touch to the recipes."

ED'S FAMOUS BLACK BEAN CASSEROLE

We heard about this dish from Anne Koch, and Mary Frank also praised Ed's culinary expertise. So even as Ed denied his ability to set a recipe down "just so," we, managed to convince him to divulge his Southwestern secrets.

1 pound black beans
1 carrot
2 stalks celery
2 cloves garlic
1 whole onion
1 ham hock
1 chili pepper, seeded and chopped **OR**
1 teaspoon hot red chili powder
1 herb bouquet (bay leaf, cumin, thyme to taste)
salt and pepper to taste
3 tablespoons lard (no substitutions here)
dry white wine
sour cream
dill

Wash, drain and pick over beans to remove any stones; soak beans overnight in cold water. Next day, in a large pot, place beans and add enough water to cover; add carrot, celery, garlic, onion, ham hock, chili pepper, spices, salt and pepper. Bring water to a boil, reduce heat, cover and simmer at very low heat until beans are almost tender (about three hours); add boiling water as needed. Do not overcook beans; remove ham hock, vegetables and herb bouquet. Preheat oven to 350°F. Place beans in large casserole and dot with lard; add salt. Pour in enough wine to cover beans and bake for 30 minutes. Serve beans with dollop of sour cream and garnish with dill, if desired.

EMPAÑADITAS DE CARNE (Mincemeat Turnovers)

A holiday treat, these turnovers burst at the seams with rich, spicy mincemeat. Serve them with a cup of Ed's Egg Nog and the winter will seem a lot shorter.

1/2 pound beef, trimmed and cubed
1/2 pound pork, trimmed and cubed
1/4 cup chopped piñon nuts
1 1/2 cup raisins
2 cups apples, peeled and finely chopped
1/4 cup candied orange **OR**
grapefruit peel
1 teaspoon cinnamon
1/2 teaspoon ground cloves
1 teaspoon ground coriander
1 cup sugar
1 teaspoon salt
2 tablespoons rum or cognac, if desired
pastry dough (see recipe)
peanut oil
confectioner s sugar

In a heavy pot, boil beef; drain, reserve some of the stock, and set aside. Boil pork until cooked; drain (make sure the pork is cooked completely.) Grind meat in food grinder or food processor; set aside. Mix nuts, raisins, apples, fruit peel and spices in large bowl and add meat. Stir in sugar, salt, rum or cognac to taste. Mixture should be firm, not runny; if more liquid is needed, use beef stock. Set filling aside. On a floured board, roll out pastry dough to an 1/8" thickness. Cut out 4" to 6" circles using a cookie or biscuit cutter (do not allow dough to rise; if it does rise after cutting, roll circles flat). Put a tablespoon of mincemeat mixture into center of each circle. Fold over dough to form half-circles and flute edges by pinching between thumb and forefinger. Let empañaditas stand for 5 minutes. Heat peanut oil in deep fryer. When fryer indicates oil is hot enough, fry empañaditas until golden brown. Drain on paper towels. Dust with confectioner s sugar and serve warm.

132

Pastry Dough

1 cake yeast
1 1/2 cups water
3 tablespoons lard (no substitutions here)
1 1/2 teaspoons salt
2 tablespoons sugar
flour

Soak yeast in small amount warm water (follow package directions.) Heat 1 1/2 cups water (do not boil), add lard, salt and sugar; stir until solids are dissolved. Cool mixture to lukewarm and add dissolved yeast. Add enough flour to make a non-sticky dough. Roll out and fill as directed above.

IMPULSIVE EGG NOG

Ed reminded us that he cooks by impulse, but this drink tastes like a lot of thought (and testing) has gone into it.

6 eggs
6 tablespoons brown sugar
1/2 teaspoon vanilla extract
4 to 6 ounces dark Jamaican rum
1/2 quart good bourbon whiskey
1/2 quart milk
1/2 quart heavy cream
grated nutmeg

Separate the eggs; set aside the yolks. Beat the egg whites until they form stiff peaks; store in refrigerator until needed. In a large bowl, beat the egg yolks with brown sugar, vanilla, rum, whiskey and milk. In a separate bowl, whip the cream until it forms stiff peaks. Using a perforated spoon, fold cream into the egg mixture; chill. Just before serving, fold in the whipped egg whites and sprinkle with a dash of nutmeg.

CHICKEN CHAVEZ

Ed recommends serving this dish accompanied by asparagus tips sautéed in butter and a bowl of polenta. He also says that "dessert should be fruit and cheese-cantaloupe, papaya, oranges, apples, or combinations of these. And avocado! Always avocado!"

1 1/2 pounds chicken breasts
1 tablespoon butter
2 tablespoons peanut oil
salt and pepper to taste
1/2 onion, peeled and chopped
2 cloves garlic, peeled and chopped
1/2 cup chopped celery
1/4 teaspoon thyme
1/4 teaspoon marjoram
2 tomatoes, peeled and chopped
1/2 cup dry white wine
1/2 cup white, seedless grapes
fresh mint, grapes or parsley for garnish

In a heavy skillet, sauté (do not brown) chicken in butter and oil. Season with salt and pepper and remove to platter. To remaining oil in pan, add onion, garlic, celery, thyme, and marjoram, and sauté for 5 minutes (do not brown); add tomatoes. Place chicken and vegetable mixture into a casserole and bake at 350°F for approximately 30 minutes, or until chicken is tender; turn chicken at least once. Remove chicken breasts and set aside; keep warm. Pour remaining liquid and vegetables into blender; blend until smooth. Pour blended sauce into saucepan, add 1/2 cup wine; cook on low heat for 10 minutes, stirring occasionally. Add grapes to sauce and cook for 5 minutes more. Return chicken to casserole, pour sauce over chicken and warm in oven. Garnish with mint, grapes, or parsley.

Betty Marks
literary agent

"If people followed my diabetic diet, they'd be far healthier."

Betty's literary clients have included Sydney H. Schanberg, whose book formed the basis for the film **The Killing Fields,** award-winning journalist Morton Mintz, author of **President Ron's Appointment Book,** and Woodstock resident Barry Ballister, whose produce includes **Barry Ballister's Fruit and Vegetable Stand.**

When Betty, a diabetic, discovered that the recipes available for her special diet were uninspiring, she decided to undertake what became **The International Menu Diabetic Cookbook.** Betty's second book, **The High-Calcium, Low-Calorie Cookbook,** is a panoply of 250 healthful low fat, low salt, sugarless recipes, proving that limited diets don't necessarily mean limited choices. "These dishes are varied, attractive and tasty," explains Betty. "In fact, if people followed my diabetic diet, they'd be far healthier!"

GUILTLESS APRICOT MOUSSE

This delicately flavored, light treat is from **The High-Calcium, Low-Calorie Cookbook** (Contemporary Books, 1987). Betty likes the mousse because it offers a way to enjoy dessert without guilt.

1/2 cup dried apricots, dried prunes or a combination
1/2 cup soft tofu (soft bean curd)
2 teaspoons pure vanilla extract
2 tablespoons nonfat dry milk
2 egg whites at room temperature
fresh mint leaves, if desired

Soak fruits in hot water for 30 minutes; drain. Drain tofu between paper towels and turn into the container of a food processor or blender, along with the fruit, vanilla and dry milk. Process. In a separate bowl, whip the egg whites until stiff but not dry. Pour fruit mixture into a bowl and fold in egg whites. Spoon mousse into dessert glasses; chill. Serve garnished with mint leaves, if desired.

135

Sonia Malkine
folksinger

"The bread in America is different."

Sonia is well-known in the Hudson Valley as a Breton folksinger complete with lacy coif. "I was born in Paris, but my ancestors came from Brittany," she explains, and in fact, she was introduced to Woodstock by a French connection. "The activist Emma Goldman was a family friend, and we often stayed at her house in St. Tropez, where we met Stella Ballantine. Later, when I came to America with my husband, George (a painter and founder of the Parisian Surrealist movement), Stella recommended that we spend summers in Woodstock at the Maverick with our four children." Within a few years, the Malkines had bought a house and moved to Woodstock permanently. "It was June of 1953," recalls Sonia; "the mountain laurel surrounding the house were in blossom and the place was beautiful." She lives in the same house and the laurel still captivate her each spring.

What does Sonia miss most about France from a culinary point of view? Bread. "The bread in America is different," she notes. "The soil, the wheat and the water must have an effect on the flavor. It's like champagne: you can make it in other parts of the world, but only the Champagne district of France has the right amount of chalk in the soil to give the right flavor to the grapes."

COQ AU VIN MALKINE

Sonia likes to make a big pot of this dish when the family gets together for dinner. "My grandmother gave me this recipe," Sonia says. "She always added prunes to soak up the heavy burgundy and add some sweetness to the sauce." As far as the amounts go, Sonia recommends tasting the sauce and adding the herbs "depending on what is lacking."

1 medium onion, sliced
butter or vegetable oil
1 medium chicken (about 5 pounds), cut up
salt and pepper to taste
1 teaspoon **each** thyme, rosemary, oregano, basil
2-3 garlic cloves
2 cups burgundy (or 1 cup wine and 1 cup water)
1/2 pound prunes
sliced mushrooms, if desired
cooked noodles, if desired

     In a heavy casserole, brown onion in butter or oil; add chicken and brown. Stir in salt and pepper to taste. Add herbs, garlic, burgundy and prunes. Bring mixture to a boil, then reduce heat and simmer until chicken is done. Add sliced mushrooms to casserole 15 minutes before it is finished cooking. Serve with noodles.

Joanne Michaels & Stuart Ober
author & financial planner

Stuart and I moved to Woodstock from New York City in 1981, a few days after I turned 30. A self-confessed whole foods devotee, I was glad to discover, at the time, three health food stores in town. What I like about Woodstock, besides its obvious attributes, is that it is a part of the American granola belt!

A PURIST'S PEANUT BUTTER & JELLY MUFFINS

Our four-year-old son, Erik, likes to bake, and he particularly enjoys inventing new recipes. This is one we came up with together.

1/2 cup butter, softened
1/2 cup old-fashioned, unblanched, smooth peanut butter (no sugar added)
1/2 cup brown sugar
1/2 cup pure honey
2 eggs
2 cups whole grain, stone ground, whole wheat flour (with no preservatives, artificial coloring, flavoring, BHA or BHT)
1 tablespoon baking powder
1/2 teaspoon salt
1 teaspoon cinnamon
1 teaspoon nutmeg
3/4 cup milk
1/2 cup fruit-only preserves, sweetened only with natural fruit juice

Preheat oven to 425°F. Cream together butter and peanut butter. Add sugar, honey and eggs; beat until light and fluffy. In a small bowl, combine flour with baking powder, salt and spices. Add to creamed mixture, alternating with milk. Stir to blend; don't beat. Place paper liners in muffin pans and fill each three-quarters of the way with batter. Put a teaspoon of preserves on top of each muffin. Bake for 20 minutes or until muffins test done. Makes about 15.

FOR THE BIRDS, FROM STUART

There is yet another Woodstock close to the hearts of America: a silly yellow bird named Woodstock who stars in the cartoon strip **Peanuts.** Hence, it is fitting that this book include a tasty morsel for the birds and it is to the local avian residents that this appropriate peanut/suet delight is dedicated!

2 cups suet
1 cup peanut butter
2 cups shelled sunflower seeds
1 cup millet
1 cup fine cracked corn
1 cup oatmeal
suet cases or twine

Place suet in a saucepan and heat until melted. Let cool, then reheat. Add peanut butter and blend well. Add the sunflower seeds, millet, corn and oatmeal and stir. Place the mixture into small plastic containers or cupcake tins and let harden. Hang in suet cases (nylon webbed sacks, available at farm and feed stores) or thread blocks with twine. The result is a dish fit for an eagle, or at least a local chickadee. (A recipe to deter raccoons, who will also love this mix, will be found in Volume 2 of **Famous Woodstock Cooks!**)

Mary Barile
author

I love food. And I love hearing from people who love food. So there wasn't a better way to spend golden summer afternoons than visiting famous Woodstock cooks and talking with them about their favorite dishes and the world in general. Since I'm not a full-time Woodstockian, I often felt like Alice in her adventures down the rabbit hole: everything <u>seemed</u> normal, but upon closer inspection people turned into green witches, dancers, 18th-century composers, Santa Claus, painters, authors and scriptwriters who created Martian invasions. When Alice woke up, she missed her "curious, wonderful" dream. Pity poor Alice; I still have Woodstock!

COLLINS' TEA BREAD

My Dublin-born grandmother loved to bake, and this moist, sweet tea bread often made its appearance on St. Patrick's Day, along with stories of the IRA and the Troubles.

1/2 cup raisins
1/2 cup hot water
1/4 cup butter
1/4 cup sugar
2 eggs
4 1/2 teaspoons baking powder
1/4 teaspoon baking soda
1/4 teaspoon salt
1 3/4 cups unsifted flour
1 cup sour cream
1 teaspoon caraway seeds
butter and raspberry jam, if desired

Preheat oven to 375°F; grease and flour an 8" round cake pan. Soak the raisins in the hot water for 5 minutes; drain and set aside. In a large bowl, cream together the butter and the sugar. Beat in the eggs, one at a time. Stir in the baking powder, baking soda and salt. Blend in the flour, alternating with the sour cream. Stir in the raisins and the caraway seeds (batter will be thick.) Spread batter in cake pan; cut a large "X" in surface of batter. Bake at 375°F for 10 minutes; reduce the heat to 350°F and bake for 30 minutes or until a toothpick inserted in the bread comes out clean. Cool for 10 minutes in the pan; serve warm with butter and raspberry jam.

ARKVILLE APPLE CAKE

This heavy, moist gingerbread with the surprise of sugared apples is from **Catskill Cookery.**

3 medium Empire apples, peeled and sliced
1/3 cup sugar mixed with 2 teaspoons cinnamon
1/4 cup shortening
1/2 cup hot water
1 cup dark molasses
2 1/2 cups flour
1 1/2 teaspoons ginger
1 teaspoon baking soda
1/2 teaspoon salt
whipped cream, if desired

Preheat over to 350°F. Thoroughly grease an 8 x 11" pan; arrange apple slices in bottom of pan and sprinkle with sugar and cinnamon mixture; set aside. In a large bowl, mix shortening with water and add molasses; set aside. In a separate bowl, sift together flour, ginger, baking soda and salt. Stir into liquid mixture and beat until batter is smooth. Pour gingerbread mixture over apples. Bake for 40-45 minutes or until a toothpick inserted in center of cake comes out clean. Invert pan onto heatproof platter; let stand 5 minutes, then carefully remove pan. Serve cake warm, with whipped cream.

About the Authors

Joanne Michaels and Mary Barile are the authors of **The Best of the Hudson Valley and Catskills** (Crown, 1988), an insider s' guide covering the best inns, restaurants, museums, and sights from Westchester to Albany.

Joanne is the author of **Living Contradictions: The Women of the Baby Boom Come of Age** (Simon & Schuster, 1982). Her byline has appeared in **Redbook, The Village Voice, Working Mother, Capital Region** and other publications. The former editor-in-chief of **Hudson Valley Magazine,** she was also an editor at St. Martin's Press. Joanne lives in Woodstock with her husband and son.

Mary is the owner of **Heritage Publications,** a small press that specializes in regional and collectible cookbooks. Recent books have included **Waffles & Wafers, Catskill Cookery** and **Funeral Pie and Old Man's Cake: Good Old-Fashioned Farm Baking.** The editor of a collectors' newsletter, **Old & New Books for Cooks,** her byline has appeared in **Early American Life, McCalls Needlework & Crafts, New York Alive** and other publications. Mary lives in Arkville, New York.

```
*************************************************
```

ORDER ADDITIONAL COPIES TODAY

```
*************************************************
```

JMB PUBLICATIONS
BOX 425
WOODSTOCK, NY 12498

Please send me _____ copies of **Famous Woodstock Cooks** at \$9.95 per copy, plus \$1.50 postage and handling for the first book and 50¢ for each additional book. Enclosed find my check or money order for \$_____.

Name _____

Address _____

City _____

State _____   **Zip** _____

```
*************************************************
```

JMB PUBLICATIONS
BOX 425
WOODSTOCK, NY 12498

Please send me _____ copies of **Famous Woodstock Cooks** at \$9.95 per copy, plus \$1.50 postage and handling for the first book and 50¢ for each additional book. Enclosed find my check or money order for \$_____.

Name _____

Address _____

City _____

State _____   **Zip** _____

```
*************************************************
```